URBAN VILLAGE, GLOBAL CITY

Gerard Lemos

With research by Sarah Kingston

Gerard Lemos is a partner at Lemos & Crane. He has published a study of mutual aid in social housing written with the distinguished sociologist Michael Young, *The Communities We Have Lost and Can Regain*. He has also published two books on dealing with racial harassment in social housing and one on fair recruitment and selection. He is the author of numerous reports and articles about social housing.

He also advises, and delivers training for, many public and voluntary organisations on implementing equality and diversity and on regenerating communities in social housing.

In the early 1980s he was one of the founders of ASRA Greater London Housing Association and was the first Director. He then worked for many years as a senior manager at Circle 33 Housing Trust in housing management and development.

He is the Director of Studies for the School for Social Entrepreneurs, chairs the Arts Council's cultural diversity committee and is a board member of Homeless International and the London International Festival of Theatre. He is a fellow of the RSA.

"For anyone trying to 'turn around' a deprived neighbourhood, this work has some important advice: don't even think about sorting things out as a 'housing' professional (or even worse, as a developer) but work with the community to improve the quality of life. According to Lemos we should consider allocations; target trouble makers; address unemployment, poverty, health and low educational achievements if we are to make our worst estate desirable places to live".

Kate Davies
Director of Housing Services, Brighton and Hove Council and Co-ordinator of Whitehawk Initiative

"The first five years of the Colville Project have been an innovatory and immensely productive time for everyone involved, not just because of what has been achieved, but also how. Gerard Lemos's book is more than a report. It is the tale of how events in North Kensington fit in with events elsewhere. Anyone interested in urban regeneration must read it, but if you are interested in how our society is changing, you are certain to enjoy this compelling and highly readable account of the life of one neighbourhood and its people."

Sarah Harrison
Community Development Manager Notting Hill Housing Group

"People who question the power of local communities to help themselves should read this book. Action to improve the environment by planting trees, to make dangerous areas safe and to banish drug dealers from the local scene are some of the achievements of the Colville community in Notting Hill. Their story is an example and an enormous encouragement to other communities."

Ken Bartlett
Advisor, Joseph Rowntree Foundation

Partners in North Kensington Urban Area Regeneration:

Colville Area Residents Federation
Notting Hill Housing Trust
Kensington Housing Trust
Royal Borough of Kensington and Chelsea
North Kensington City Challenge
Metropolitan Police Notting Hill

First published in Great Britain in 1998
by the Colville Project, Notting Hill
Housing Trust and Lemos&Crane.

Colville Project
108 Talbot Road
London W11 1JR

Notting Hill Housing Trust
Grove House
27 Hammersmith Grove
London W6 0JL

ISBN Number 1-898001-58-8

A CIP catalogue record for this book is
available from the British Library

Cover, text design and setting by
dap ltd, London

Printed by Redwood Books, Trowbridge

Contents

Acknowledgements   *vii*

Foreword   *ix*

Map of the Colville estate   *xi*

Chapter one
Urban village, global city   *1*

Chapter two
108 – The Village Shop   *17*

Chapter three
The kingdom of individuals   *29*

Chapter four
In the public places   *51*

Chapter five
Mutual communities   *67*

Chapter six
Arrival, struggle, inclusion – The question of race   *81*

Chapter seven
Two villages: The local economy   *91*

Chapter eight
Sustaining the impact – The Mutual Aid Compact   *99*

Chapter nine
Lessons learnt   *105*

Chapter ten
To conclude   *115*

Appendix A
Key achievements of the Colville Project   *119*

Bibliography   *121*

Index   *123*

Acknowledgements

A special place has already been given to Sarah Kingston on the title page for researching the material for this book. Her sense of fun, as well as the more common research virtues of thoroughness and precision, makes her a great person to work with. My greatest gratitude to her. I want also to thank local residents and business people in Colville and the rest of North Kensington for the time they spent with us in interviews and focus groups. Their insights, observations and descriptions contributed more to my understanding of the flavour and the mood of the neighbourhood and its history than any amount of data could. The staff at 108 Talbot Road, Sarah Harrison, Nivene Powell, Neil Stubberfield, Anne Gomez and Frank Russell were all enormously enthusiastic and helpful with the project, giving generously of their time and their ideas. Katherine Rogers had the thankless task of transcribing the tapes of focus groups. Nivene Powell was a source of fascinating information, insight and wisdom. I want to thank them all.

The staff of Notting Hill Housing Trust also should be thanked. Ros Spencer commissioned the work and supported it throughout. Sue Black and Peter Redman gave lots of encouragement and support. Their interest in the ideas and suggestions being made was highly motivating. Both Ros Spencer and Sarah Harrison made helpful (and amusing) observations about the drafts. Sarah Harrison guided the writing of this book from start to finish gently and persistently. I am greatly in all their debt.

At Lemos & Crane, Eileen Hodges and Gill Goodby performed a tireless and methodical job with the editing, always with good humour and I am grateful for that.

Whilst many people deserve thanks for contribution, oftentimes unsung, responsibility for mistakes and misinterpretations remain solely with the author. Similarly, the views expressed are mine alone.

Foreword

The Colville Project opened and closed on much the same theme – whether or not the Residents Information Centre, the Village Shop, was needed.

Five years ago, I took on the residents..., and lost. 'Why on earth,' I reasoned, 'when the Trust has an area office two minutes walk away, do we need another one?' And anyway, (here was the clincher) I didn't have a budget for it.

At that early stage we all learnt an important lesson. For my part I learned that the Project's base was not about geography or distance so much as it was about the symbolism of independence from any established institution. Like a parent nurturing a child I had to accept that Colville Project had to be allowed the freedom to become what it would become.

Residents for their part learned that if something was worth fighting for, they should not allow themselves to be browbeaten by well-intentioned bureaucrats telling them they couldn't have it because there was no budget.

What follows is an account of the life of a project of which residents should be rightly proud. This book tells a great and heartening story. It is written with verve and optimism. There are many lessons for all the agencies involved in the project and indeed for everyone engaged in urban regeneration. The Colville Project has come of age and it is my hope and belief that the future of the Village Shop at 108 will be secured through the continuing determination of residents who made Colville Project so much more than I ever dreamed it would be.

Ros Spencer
Area Director, Notting Hill Housing Trust

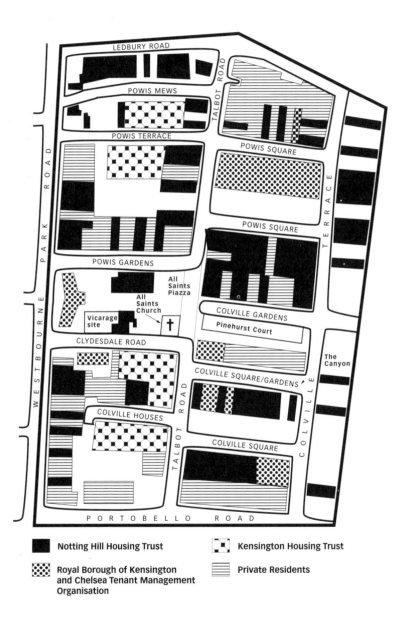

Colville Estate

With trunk tucked up compactly –
The elephant's sign of defeat –
He resisted, but is the child of reason now.
His straight trunk seems to say:
When what we hoped for came to nothing,
We revived.

Elephants,
Marianne Moore

Chapter one
Urban village, global city

The vicissitudes of time

Many people say and more people feel that God made the country and people made the cities. Even if it is only people who made earthly cities, earthly cities hint at and evoke the heavenly city. Vermeer's wonderful painting 'View of Delft' is superficially an unassuming low, horizontal, red-brick townscape punctuated by towers and spires across a wide shimmering river. On our side of the river are two tiny, black-clad figures. Above the townscape is a North European blue sky fading to white clouds and darker rain clouds lifting. But such a prosaic description denies the power of the painting, imbued with the light that only the Dutch master has ever created.

Vermeer has taken the bare facts of the city and, without manipulation, rendered them transcendent. That city shining out at us across the water is Delft, but it is also the heavenly Jerusalem, the city of peace. The variety of the skyline of the buildings is profound but not extravagant - towers, churches and houses, sunlit swathes and areas in mellow shadows. We are the tiny figures on the near quayside, looking across at the earthly city but yearning for the holy city.

And this interplay of the eternal and the mutable, the sublime and the mundane, has always mobilised the drama of life in the city. The most evocative of travel writers, Jan Morris, has described cities as "those most fascinating of all creations of human energy and ingenuity."

Cities have never stood still. They have always been engines of change and receivers for change. Thomas More, Henry VIII's Catholic Lord Chancellor who lived all his life in London and eventually lost his life for his religion, wrote many times in the 1500s that there is no eternal city. If God is universal and immutable but human nature has fallen from

1

grace the places where we live our temporal lives are just antechambers for eternity. What goes on in these antechambers can, indeed must, change constantly as we attempt to live lives of redemption and atonement. St. Augustine draws our attention to this same urban mutability in his City of God. In Augustine's work the history of the world is conceived in terms of two cities, the city of the World and the city of God, distinct but not entirely separate, together experiencing 'the vicissitudes of time'.

In our times a new role for the city has been borne of great political, economic and social shifts, the combination of which have never occurred simultaneously before. The relative decline in the importance of war in our part of the world, if not in others, is tilting the balance. Nations and empires are seen as less crucial unifying factors than regions, cities and even neighbourhoods. As Geoff Mulgan has put it,

> "If territory is a less reliable source of power than connections, then the city comes back into its own. Many of its neutral characteristics - the emphasis on the exterior of the human personality, on change and on tolerance... - become economic as well as social values. And far from being made obsolete by communications technologies, the cities characterised as centres of sociability become more important because...each programmed interaction needs to be backed by an unprogrammed one, a less formal interchange in a bar, a restaurant or someone's home. Trade, exchange and cities all thrive amidst connexity."

How are cities made?

Cities are places where large numbers of people have come together to live, to trade, not just amongst themselves, but with as many other people as possible, all over the world they know. Cities have also always been centres of producing goods and services and they are often seats of government, sometimes for their regions, or their countries, or even empires.

Once large numbers of people have come together to live cheek by jowl, their shared and individual experiences elide and collide to produce an efforescence in music, literature, theatre and the visual arts or in their modern equivalents – film, television, multi-media. Things that people want to do together - religious worship, sports and leisure - all become achievable. Whatever your interests, you are likely to find many others who share them in the city.

Chronicles of the impending death of cities have been much foretold and much exaggerated. Cities continue to be the most dynamic places to live for millions of people across the planet. In 1900 only one tenth of the world's population lived in cities. Half of the world's population will live in cities by the year 2000. In thirty years' time it may rise to as much as three-quarters. Much of this growth will be in the cities of the developing world – Jakarta, Bombay, and Dhakar.

Having been the most populous city in the world in 1939, London saw its population decline markedly in the period up to the early 1980s. In some parts of inner London the population has been falling since the 19th century. But even in London it is now rising again by about 20,000 people a year. In the late 1990s it stands at just below 7 million, virtually the same as New York City. Projections suggest that this growth will continue. London is still attracting new residents, both rich and poor, from Britain and elsewhere.

London, uniquely of the great cities, combines all the qualities of great cities – production, services, centre of government, culture, trade, a natural strategic location on the river Thames, a geographical hub between America and Europe and, in the post-colonial era, a magnet for people from Africa, the Caribbean, South Asia and South East Asia, escaping oppression or in search of prosperity.

Global cities

International competition between cities to attract the best jobs, companies, sports and cultural events has led some commentators to suggest world class cities are becoming decoupled from their hinterland, referring more and more to one another for comparison and identity, not to the national identities and cultures of which they form a geographical part. You will see in most international cities international shops, airlines, banks, companies and brands. So if Barcelona can have the Olympics, so can we in...wherever. The European central bank must not be allowed to take business in financial services from the City of London. And if Paris can have gigantic improvements to their museums and galleries, so must we. We are not a world class city unless we have an opera house which can afford Pavarotti. And so on.

Global cities are a still developing modern trend. Non-capital cities like Manchester and Birmingham aspire to this status. London unquestionably has it, as it has since the nineteenth century, as does New York. But global cities are not a wholly new phenomenon. Defined as cities which link to social, economic and cultural activity across the known world, they have existed since the earliest cities – Mohenjodaro in Pakistan, which is 4,500 years old, Tikal in Guatemala, which had its heyday in about AD250 and Teotichuacan in Mexico in AD600. The latter two, now deserted ruins, all dominated their whole world even if their whole world was geographically rather less than our known world. In Europe we have more familiar, and more recent antecedents for global cities in Athens, Rome and Venice. I shall be arguing here that global economic forces affect all neighbourhoods in the city, including Colville, the subject of our attention in this book, in different ways, not all positive.

We live say some in an Age of Insecurity or an Age of Anxiety. The Catalan sociologist, Manuel Castells, has charted the seismic shifts we are currently living through in the social and economic geology more acutely than either the gung ho free marketeers or the prophets of doom. He expressed his concerns about globalisation and its result, the network society, in the *New Statesman* on 5 June 1998,

> "This network society I describe has an extraordinary dynamism. At the same time, by combing the globe ceaselessly for things of value, it excludes everything, and everyone, not of value. And those excluded are not just those in third world countries; they are in the South

Bronx or in Tower Hamlets or Naples. It has the potential to become the most exclusionary system in history, while also possessing the potential to be the most productive system in history."

I shall in the pages to come have much to say about the divisive impact of these changes in our look at Colville. And I shall also, towards the end of the book, make some suggestions about how these excluding impacts could be ameliorated, how people could be offered more than, as Stevie Wonder put it, "living just enough for the city".

Urban villages

Because we have modern global cities that have much in common, we cannot conclude that they are much alike. Homogeneity has, in this context, strict limits. London is unique. Paradoxically, globalisation is giving us global cities again but it is not giving rise to global government or global living. Small is still, for most people, beautiful. Indeed globalisation is making people 'act local', even while they 'think global'. Increasingly the daily skirmishes of globalisation are being played out not at international summit conferences or in conglomerate boardrooms, but in town halls, community projects and at conferences about innovation and entrepreneurship in small, local businesses. A new wave of social concerns and a growing desire for community spirit have come in the wake of economic change. Once preoccupied primarily with economic issues, the public is more and more concerned about social issues. Once focused primarily on the competitiveness of large-business corporations, leaders in Britain and elsewhere are more and more concerned about the strength of families and communities and the competitiveness of cities, states and regions. Hence in Britain, we have a Social Exclusion Unit to co-ordinate Government policy and we are to have devolution to Scotland, Wales and possibly Northern Ireland. London is to have a Mayor. The other big cities are likely to follow. All the regions are to have regional development agencies. We know that we need changes in the institutional structures and processes of government if we are to respond competitively and cohesively to these paradoxical changes.

Being more global making us concerned about being more local is played out more dramatically in London than in any other big city. Along with the unique combination of all the great features of city life, London has one uniquely its own and almost uniquely English – the urban village. Other cities have them too. But because London is an ancient city, nowhere has them in as great a number or complexity. And it was ever so. Abercrombie's visionary plan for London, written in 1943, and never fully implemented (indeed still too frequently ignored) saw London for what it was:

"The casual observer or map reader is apt to be left with the impression that London is just one immense urban agglomeration broken up here and there by open spaces, industrial areas and railways, but otherwise a mixture of roads and buildings of all sizes and uses which need only be considered as part of London's great sprawl. It is this impression which in the past has led to many reconstruction proposals that completely ignore the local conditions or civic pride of a particular district.

A more careful study of the structure of London reveals a highly organised and inter-related system of communities as one of its main characteristics. These communities are grouped organically around the heart of London – the Port, the City and the West End. This characteristic is perhaps more peculiar to London than to any other capital city in the world, for the generally low density of its two or three-storey development. Combined with its extensive area, it has created a need for numerous subsidiary civic and commercial centres. In other cities the development has usually been of a more intense character, in which the city centre and multi-storey block buildings dominate."

Many urban villages in London can be traced back to the original villages that existed when the capital was smaller than present day Southampton. Others have been determined by local geographical conditions or artificial barriers, such as railways, canals and industrial activities, often now fallen into desuetude. The roads and railways, not recognising the existence of communities, cut straight across their centres as we can see all over West London.

Community groupings in these urban villages help in no small measure towards the inculcation of local pride. They facilitate organisation and control and they are the means of defining and resolving what would otherwise be unappealing and interminable aggregations of housing – distant barracks far from work and fun which too easily become wastelands of the supposedly free.

Each community has its own schools, public houses, public buildings, community meeting places, shops, open spaces, churches and so on. Perhaps the most important of these, for reasons I shall go on to describe in Chapter five, is the primary school. It is the growing heart of the community, embodying its hope for the future and the epicentre of many social networks for adults as well as children, which survive long after the children have left the primary school and perhaps even the neighbourhood.

And the urban village is, we are told, to have a new lease of life. Close by the Millennium Dome in Greenwich there is to be a new village and others are planned too. They have as much appeal as ever they did. The former diplomat and environmentalist, Sir Crispin Tickell, spoke for the many not the few in the simplest terms when he told the *Financial Times* on 6th June 1998, "My ambition would still be to go somewhere where there was a good school, a good community, a share in a communal garden and not too much crime."

I am concerned here not with new villages but that we should not lose those urban villages we already have; the ones, like Colville, that display those characteristics listed above.

A backdrop of social change

In this opening piece I have, in a rhetorical way, set two trends against one another – the move towards a global city versus the maintenance of the urban village. In reality, of course, they are less contradictory than they seem. The whole of human history is characterised by the constant wish to innovate while simultaneously maintaining and sustaining tradition and habit. It is those two omnipresent forces, the former creating the global city and the latter maintaining the urban village, each destructive without the other, that are at play here as they are at play everywhere. In the forthcoming chapters I will seek to set events in Colville in the last five years against the backdrop of local, citywide, national and international social changes. I want to show if I can how some of these forces have affected the lives of neigbourhoods, individuals and families. Without seeing the backdrop, events in the foreground make little sense. We are cast as blindfolded actors making up the lines as we go along on a constantly moving stage set. And so it is to the Colville foreground I now turn.

The history of Colville

Here is Roy Porter from his magisterial study of London's social history:

> "East of Wormwood Scrubs Notting Dale was popularly known as the 'piggeries and potteries' (there were said to be over 3,000 pigs and 1,000 humans). Conditions were described by the sanitary reformer Edwin Chadwick as 'filthy in the extreme', while Dickens portrayed it as 'a plague spot scarcely equalled in insalubrity by any other part of London'. Its largely Irish inhabitants (many settling after eviction from slums knocked down to make way for railways) squeezed a living from pig-keeping, brickmaking, street selling and laundry. Squalid lodging-houses and furnished rooms abounded, with one public house for every twenty-five dwellings. As late as the 1890s, half the children born in the district died in their first year.

Yet but a mile to the south-east, Notting Hill scored. The Hippodrome racecourse built there in 1837, north of the Portobello Road, proving a flop, it was replaced by the striking Ladbroke estate, its axis being Ladbroke Grove, its centre St John's Church. The superior gardens and squares constructed west of Kensington Park Road and north as far as Elgin Crescent attracted paired villas set in picturesque crescents. 'Leafy Ladbroke' spread east towards Bayswater and south of Westbourne Grove to include by the 1860s Chepstow Villas, Pembridge Villas and Pembridge Square. Kensington Park became a district of handsome houses.

The development petered out towards the north, however. By the mid-1860s housebuilding for the wealthy had outrun demand, and Ladbroke Grove stopped short south of where the Hammersmith and City Line was soon to run. Buildings off the beaten track, around Colville and Powis Squares, were unlucky from the start, being among the first in Kensington to be sliced up into multiple occupancy, declining by the 1870s into lodgings and bedsits."

A walk around Colville

The Colville estate is the nucleus of Colville ward bounded by Westbourne Park Road to the north, Colville Terrace to the south, Portobello Road to the west and Ledbury Road to the east. By defining and drawing an imaginary line around its perimeter the neighbourhood assumes some of the characteristics of a council estate, despite its rather grand historical appearance of tall stucco-ed, portico-ed houses – hence the use of the word 'estate' in popular shorthand. The word 'estate' may have been intended to convey something rather more aristocratic when the area was built. The word has stuck. Its meaning has changed.

Approaching from Ledbury Road and walking towards Portobello Road down Talbot Road, the main road running from east to west, you pass local shops - an electrical shop, 'My Beautiful Launderette', a shop selling snacks and

9

sandwiches and Serge's corner shop. Further down there is a locksmith, a shop selling classic (not classical) records and CDs. These shops service the needs of less well off local people. As one resident told us "The launderette is very busy. That's a sure sign that many people around here don't have much money."

On the other side of Talbot Road is an extremely modern, fashionable and expensive restaurant, built in a completely refurbished pub, Dakota. There is also Coins, a less upmarket, but also fashionable café. Some of the buildings have been redesigned in the most minimal, downlit modern fashion as offices for model agencies, graphic designers and media companies providing high added value services, not manufacturing products; that very range of new activities Manuel Castells was pointing to. Services are delivered from here not to local people, but to the rest of London and beyond; across the world indeed. With this combination of fashion, eating, shopping and small service businesses the modern urban economy is on view just in Talbot Road, alongside the service providing local shops I have already described. And some of the people that work in these new businesses are not to everyone's taste. The *Observer* newspaper commented in April 1998 "Trustafarians – the irritating video brats and furniture designers have laid siege to this part of West London in recent years...baseball caps and mobile phones." Trustafarian is an elision of 'trust-fund babes', carefree young people of independent means and the more traditional Rastafarians of the Notting Hill neighbourhood.

Walking on beyond the shops down Talbot Road you reach All Saints Piazza. On one side of the piazza is the elegant and beautifully lit Victorian stone church, with its rising belfry, a small masterpiece of Victorian architecture. The building of the church was completed in 1860, ten years before the houses in the nearby streets. It is built in the Gothic style of the fourteenth century, much beloved by Victorian followers of Giles Gilbert Scott. The belfry, wide, octagonal and supported by flying buttresses 'contains much constructional colour'. The main body of the church is unusually lofty. Each of the transepts has distinctive rose windows. Built of yellow Bath stone, the church is a highly distinctive landmark.

But by 1992 the piazza outside it had become an eyesore, as I will go on to describe in Chapter four. Remodelling it has been a key priority and, environmentally, a corner stone of the work of the last five years. Carrying on along Talbot Road large Victorian stucco-ed houses, painted white, cream and yellow, seven or eight storeys high with pillared porticoes, are interspersed with modern 1970s blocks of flats, built to replace Victorian terraced housing, in hindsight with some regret. Whilst not every lost building should be replaced as it was, where it was, a more harmonious solution could have been found. But the disrespectful attitudes of the then architectural fashions meant that low rise, brick built unadorned blocks of flats won the day, with little aesthetic regard, except for height, to those buildings they abutted.

The height and colour of the older houses give them a grand and flamboyant air, which was belied soon after they were built by the conditions within them as Roy Porter noted. Off Talbot Road to the left there are two small town squares surrounded by these large houses – Powis Square and Colville Square.

Colville in 1992

By 1992 Colville was the most densely populated ward in London - 10,000 people lived in the ward. On census night in 1991, 202 people were living on every hectare, compared with the average for Greater London of 42 and Inner London of 78. The population of the ward increased by 7 per cent between 1981 and 1991. Colville was also the ward in Kensington and Chelsea with the highest percentage of children under 16 living with one adult, again well above the average for Inner London. There were more dependent children living in what was then classed as unsuitable accommodation in Colville than anywhere else in the borough – 93 per cent, as compared with an Inner London average of 58 per cent. The highest proportion of unemployed 16 – 19 years olds in London was in Colville – 42 per cent.

The relative poverty of the people in the neighbourhood was matched by the state of the housing they lived in. Some of it had been improved in the late 1960s and early 1970s, once it had been wrested from the grasp of private landlords by the housing trusts as I shall describe in Chapter three. But by the early 1990s it was in urgent need of upgrading. Quite apart from the wear and tear of 15 years of use, standards of the 1960s and 1970s are no longer acceptable in the 1990s as I will also discuss in Chapter three. The public spaces too of Colville and Powis Square and All Saints Piazza were no longer either public or congenial. Like so many public, municipally maintained spaces, the town squares had become unloved and scruffy and so they came to attract those who are also largely unloved and scruffy - winos and junkies. Their arrival completed the disinterest of locals in using these gardens, which had been 'liberated' from private ownership in the 1970s in a swell of local idealism, either for leisure or pleasure. Crime on the street and in the home was rife, significantly exacerbated by poor standards of security to the front street doors and communal areas. Traffic flowed at some speed down rat runs, terrorising local residents, particularly children and old people. So a great deal needed to change. All of this will be described in more detail in Chapter four. Colville had become one of the most difficult places to live in London, so much so that 35.5 per cent of the tenants of social landlords had announced their intention to leave by seeking a transfer to another neighbourhood. Conversely, its trendy appeal also made it a hugely desirable area to live and stay for those renting in the private sector and paying top-of-the-market flat prices.

These oxymoronic juxtapositions are a more or less continuous theme in this discourse, and they are, as I have said, evidence of seismic global changes.

City Challenge

The City Challenge programme, launched by Michael Heseltine in 1991, marked an important shift in urban policy, not least because it took greater account of the need to address social conditions in cities, in addition to economic and physical environmental concerns. City Challenge gave a potential leadership role to the Local Authority, required public, private and voluntary partnership, focused on closely defined geographical areas and consolidated a number of initiatives into a single funding strand. Bringing these different strands and objectives together was a recognition that, as David Donnison has observed, "Social reform is a process, not an event: a kind of drama."

City Challenge was a strategic and targeted approach implemented by multi-disciplinary teams. These were all pluses. Thirty-one areas including North Kensington were awarded City Challenge status. But the City Challenge programme has attracted criticism too.

City Challenge funding was allocated not on the traditional basis of 'need' defined through a salad of statistical and other indicators, but by competition, thereby encouraging imaginative proposals. This was fine for the winners, but left the losers with hopes raised high and then summarily dashed. The narrow geographical focus has meant high impact in the defined areas, not just from public money but also private money levered in. But it has made it more difficult to make connections with regional and national economic patterns and themes. The partnership approach, while necessary and welcome, has not always been an equal partnership. The voluntary sector in particular has found that its loud voice did not compensate for the shortcomings of its poor and ad hoc financing. Alongside local authorities and TECs, their rather paltry resources leave voluntary organisations feeling like poor but noisy cousins. The involvement of local people in the process of designing and implementing City Challenge has also varied. Finally, and significantly, City Challenge has had two of the failings of many of its antecedents in urban policy – unsustainable short-termism and inadequate levels of funding.

North Kensington City Challenge

In spring 1993, North Kensington City Challenge was launched as one of the seven successful bids in London. It was a partnership of the Royal Borough of Kensington and

Chelsea, local businesses and community organisations with interests in North Kensington. It covered an area of 216 hectares at the northern tip of the borough and contained a multi-ethnic population of 26,000 people. Funding was primarily provided by Central Government at a standard City Challenge level of £37.5 million for a five year period. Other sources of funds come on stream too, from, for example, the Housing Corporation. Over the five-year period the £37.5 million of government money has attracted £127 million from other sources.

The objectives of North Kensington City Challenge were "...to create a major and permanent improvement in North Kensington [and] create London's first successful multi-cultural community".

The City Challenge investment was targeted on four objectives:

- **Improving housing** – to improve over 5,000 flats and houses in the area, with public areas of blocks of flats as a priority and creating over 390 new homes;

- **Preventing crime** – to secure over 4,000 homes with measures ranging from new fencing to improved windows and locks;

- **Investing in arts, the environment and community facilities** – to provide a variety of new youth community facilities, improve sports and leisure services, environmental improvement schemes and an arts development programme;

- **Reducing unemployment** – to invest in creating jobs by supporting existing businesses and starting up new businesses, increasing training opportunities and assisting job seekers in pursuing employment options.

The underlying ethos was to "...inspire the community with the self confidence to realise its underlying potential."

The purpose of the book

Having set a little of the social and historical context, I want to evaluate the impact of the last five years of the Colville Project based at 108 Talbot Road, one of City Challenge's 'flagship' projects. More than that, I am seeking to look not just at physical impacts, but less tangible things like the quality of people's lives, their relationships with their different landlords and with each other. I want also to draw the beginnings of a map for future activity, building on all that has already occurred. So I am seeking to look not just at measurable outcomes, important though these undoubtedly are, but I want also to convey a sense of how what has been done and what could be done can connect to wider changes in the city, in the economy and in society. It would be too easy, though appealing, to say we want more of what we have had for the last five years. Who would ask for less? I am looking for a wider and clearer context to answer the question whither now?

The structure of the book

Perhaps the most important aspect of the Colville Project was the Residents Information Centre at 108 Talbot Road. It is the work done from there that I describe in Chapter two. One of the prime motivators for the City Challenge bid was the poor state of much of the social housing in the area. So the impact of the Colville project on domestic interiors is discussed in Chapter three. Stepping out of a hopefully newly painted front door, the next consideration in the mind of a local resident is the public space. How has the environment in the neighbourhood changed? I discuss this in Chapter four. Because the public space is still generally where people meet, this leads us to whether the community has been strengthened in these last years and, if so, how? This I discuss in Chapter five. Then I look at one of the most marked features of the area - the racial and cultural diversity of the people in the neighbourhood both historically and currently, in Chapter six. In Chapter seven I look at economic changes in the neighbourhood brought about with some assistance from the Colville Project. In Chapter eight I seek to answer the question where do we go from here in Colville? How can the impact be sustained? And the lessons learnt are summarised in Chapter nine before conclusions are drawn in Chapter ten.

Chapter two
108 – The Village Shop

Traditionally many people would have lived and worked in an urban village. In shops and local businesses people would have provided the service they were paid for, but would also have offered much besides - advice, support, a friendly ear, a watchful eye, perhaps a little informal counselling. So the postman would not have just delivered the mail, he might also have noticed any vandalism or breakages. The milkman would have noticed milk not taken in from the doorstep and wondered if there was anything wrong. The person behind the counter in the post office would have known a little, or perhaps a lot, about the life of the people they were serving. The head teacher might previously have been a neighbour. They would not have had to give your child a letter expressing concern about their behaviour. They would have told you themselves.

Now it might be a different postman or postwoman everyday delivering mail by van. Lacking familiarity with the neighbourhood and its residents, they would not notice, nor act upon, any changes in the neighbourhood. People no longer have milk delivered and you are likely to go into a main post office, perhaps far from where you live and almost certainly you will be served by a stranger. And the teacher will drive to work from their home elsewhere.

Those contacts, those neighbourly concerns, that familiarity, the sense of connectedness to a local person more knowledgeable and wiser than yourself who had some concern for your welfare and a willingness to be an advocate on your behalf – most of these connections are gone. Children and older people feel the passing most acutely. Contentment of the young and the old are always hallmarks of strong community spirit. In early life and later life people value most the regular and the familiar. In adulthood, particularly amongst young adults, anonymity, variety and fashion, which are all close cousins in urban life, have greater appeal. Fashion amongst peers replaces tradition passed down the generations

17

as the principle means of learning how society is, and why it is as it is. When it comes to the extent of our range of contacts, we want our lives to be diamond-shaped, as shown below.

Figure 1: Contact networks through the lifecycle

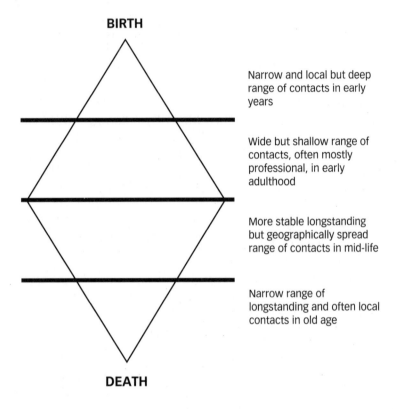

Narrow and local but deep range of contacts in early years

Wide but shallow range of contacts, often mostly professional, in early adulthood

More stable longstanding but geographically spread range of contacts in mid-life

Narrow range of longstanding and often local contacts in old age

The re-opening of a village shop

It is hard to see the sense of local people all living and working locally with people they know being restored. Nor, given the fluid structures of our modern society and economy, and the imperatives it creates to network widely, would it necessarily be desirable. Nonetheless, the local, the familiar, the concerned are still needed. These are not available at the out of town superstore. The village shop needs a modern reincarnation.

To begin with in 1993 the staff of the Colville Project were based at the offices of Notting Hill Housing Trust in All Saints' Road, offering local residents a once a week advice and information session about the project. The residents however had different ideas. They argued that, if Notting Hill Housing Trust really believed in working across tenures with residents who might be tenants of other private or social landlords or may be owner occupiers, they had to come out of Notting Hill's offices and into the community. Colville Area Residents' Federation campaigned successfully to persuade Notting Hill to acquire a local shop front in the heart of the Colville estate to establish a centre for local people - The Residents' Information Centre, 108 Talbot Road, or 108 as it quickly became known. The development of 108 as a visible, independent centre, at arms' lengths from local landlords and with a brief to look at all the needs of all local residents, not just housing and not just for tenants, captured the imagination of the community. Over the years it has become the heart of the Colville community.

At first it was a place to display plans for consultation and to hold meetings about them. In time the range of activities grew. 108 is not a community centre. It is, as I have suggested, more like a village shop, but it is not the usual range of groceries that are bought here. Instead, local residents and businesses can 'buy', though they do not pay for, help with housing improvements, upgrading the local environment, energy efficiency in the home and setting up new businesses. In return they might, if they feel they can, put some time into planning changes to the areas from which everyone benefits, either by attendance at meetings or by helping out with community activities and at local events and celebrations. The more keen could become involved in committees and local groups. Residents could get involved in the running of 108. A sub-group of Colville Area Council – the 108 management group – was formed to oversee the development and the running of the centre. And there were other ways people could do their bit. One local resident came in weekly to water the plants; another came in to give advice on the local area. The Chairs of all the residents' associations have keys for 108 and the cleaner is a local tenant. The web of local ownership and control of the centre is woven formally and informally.

Paying for 108

The local landlords, Notting Hill Housing Trust, Royal Borough of Kensington and Chelsea and Kensington Housing Trust, funded the rent and running costs of the centre and the refurbishment was carried out by Women's Education in Building (WEB) for costs only. Works were funded by City Challenge and sponsorship was provided by local businesses. Donations were made of shelving, noticeboards, the central heating system, computers, carpets right down to the doormat. Many local businesses have continued to support the activities at 108 over the years, most recently the Multi-Cultural History Week in June 1998, which is to be described in Chapter six.

Opening 108

108 opened in May 1994 and it has manifold importance in the minds of the residents. It is a symbol representing a united community, not divided by tenure, poverty and wealth, race or by any other arbitrary and emotive factors. It also represents an important victory - the residents fought for it and won it. So they felt they 'owned' it. 108 is seen as independent and holistic, not in thrall to any of the landlords, and not solely concerned with the business of managing housing. It is a space for residents, not just to air concerns and grievances, but to contribute, as I have said.

Empowerment is a much over-used word, but it seems a pertinent description of the relationship that residents have with 108.

Services from 108

Around 8,000 visits were made by local residents to 108 between May 1994 and March 1998. They asked for advice on the Colville Project City Challenge programme, on the local area, on housing and other benefits, housing management matters, rubbish collection, the environment, problems with neighbours, traffic calming, funding for community projects, training courses and seminars preparing people for employment, contacts and to attend meetings. As well as information and advice offered to individuals, local groups also sought and got help from 108. The staff at 108 did not seek to provide an in-depth or ongoing service. Their role was more to support individuals, residents' groups and campaigns, highlighting area issues and advising about the best specialist agencies.

I met with groups of tenants of all the social landlords in order to write this book. The vast majority told me how much they valued 108. They would very much regret it if it were to close. The personal service from knowledgeable people known well to those seeking advice is greatly treasured. The constancy and the familiarity of the staff is seen as crucial. Tenants commented on how frequently housing officers at the landlords' offices changed. The whole story had to be repeated each time a new person started. They also appreciate not having to make appointments to see people at 108 and not being kept waiting in an unfriendly reception area when they came for advice or help.

I was told that the staff at 108 have more time for local residents. They also work as a team, sharing information and ideas, so that all staff are known by the tenants and fairly well abreast of what's been going on without it having to be tediously or painfully repeated. Too often when tenants visited other offices, the housing management staff they wanted to see were either out or on a training course with their phones on voice mail. At 108 there is always someone available to help who you know and who knows you. They are also frustrated by the number of occasions that computer failures make it impossible for their query to be dealt with. The service at 108 is also said by tenants to be more efficient and effective. The staff know who to talk to in the institutions and how to make things happen. I was given examples of people who had been told that their flat would not be centrally heated coming into 108 and, after an intervention by 108 staff with the landlord, the decision being reversed. In short, it is not just advice that is being given, but advocacy.

The services offered by 108 are also more holistic and person-centred. People have received help in dealing with utilities, paying bills or finding work. The focus is not exclusively on housing matters. The tenants feel strongly that they would be given short shrift if they raised some of the issues with their landlords that they raised with the staff at 108.

To summarise: from the resident point of view you are likely to get help from someone you know when you want it, and the person helping is likely to be able to make something happen.

Two examples will illustrate the difference between what I have just described and the services offered in the standard way by a one-service office, operating in a way that seems to the local resident like a hermetically sealed silo.

A mother was taking her child to the primary school. They started to cross Ledbury Road. A car, going much faster than it should have been, gave the five-year-old a glancing blow. Fortunately no lasting physical injury was caused. But the incident gravely upset the child and the mother. They came into 108 immediately, frightened and anxious. One of the staff spent time with them, gave them a cup of tea, helped them to calm down and talk about what had happened. The member of staff did not say that there was nothing she could do, nor that she had another meeting to go to. After a while she gave them a leaflet about the Ledbury Road Traffic Campaign (which I will say more about in Chapter five) of which they have been active members ever since.

To take another example: a young man who was not

getting on well with his family, moved into a housing association flat. Without a job or much money, he fell behind with his rent. He stayed at home all day playing music at a volume that his neighbours regarded as a nuisance. So, in conventional housing management terms he was a problem tenant, in rent arrears and causing a nuisance. But the underlying or 'upstream' problem was that he had no work, and so no money and too much time. The solution? A member of staff at 108 asked him what kind of work he would be interested in. Youth and community work was his reply. So, through personal contacts of hers at the Council, she arranged for him to do some voluntary work. This led to paid sessional work for which he showed enthusiasm, commitment and something of a natural gift. With these qualities it was not long before he applied for and got a full-time job.

There are some powerful lessons here for mainstream housing management, in and out of the urban regeneration context:

- Tenants want a holistic, person-centred service.

- Tenants want continuity of familiar staff working as a well-informed and flexible team.

- Tenants want friendly, comfortable offices.

- Tenants want minimal use of appointments and voice mail.

108 Bulletin

A newsletter was initiated to keep local residents informed about all the projects and activities going on in the neighbourhood as well as providing a monthly calendar of events and meetings at 108. It became the place to look for what was going on. Residents, local workers and community groups were kept informed without having to attend endless meetings; but if they did want to come to a meeting they could find about it in the newsletter. For example, it was from an article in the bulletin that the 27 trees were 'adopted' by local residents, as I shall go on to describe in Chapter four. Articles about the improvements to Powis Square helped bring 70 residents out to a public meeting. I will recount that eventful occasion in more detail in Chapter four. Many of them had not previously been involved. Eighty local black people attended reminiscence evenings and two planning meetings held at Coins for the Black History Week in June 1998. They were responding to items in the newsletter.

The newsletter also became the story of the Colville Project told in monthly instalments; an archive for the project; a way of receiving, holding and managing knowledge. A kind of Pickwick Papers.

A structure for community involvement

For community involvement to be successful it needs more than a physical space. It also needs a structure. So, for example, in Walsall in the Midlands, where they have had funds both from City Challenge and from the Single Regeneration Budget, they established small neighbourhood committees and in November 1997 the first mini-local elections were held. Each committee has about 30 seats; each member is elected from about 50 households and has to live on that particular patch to avoid entryism. They have chosen which families need new central heating first and which local spots are most in need of upgrading. The first committees tended to be run by people already active in the community – vicars, community nurses, a lollipop lady, for instance. But as time has gone on new people have become involved. Some had never before been to a meeting. An alternative approach to local involvement and accountability was taken at Colville.

Colville Area Council

One of Michael Heseltine's primary objectives in establishing City Challenge was to ensure that businesses, local residents and community and voluntary organisations worked together. In Colville, firstly, there are the local residents' associations. There is one for private residents, both tenants of private landlords and owner-occupiers. Then there is the Black and Minority Ethnic Residents Group, the enormously significant work of which I will discuss in Chapter six. Tenants of each of the social landlords have residents groups – Notting Hill

Housing Trust, Kensington Housing Trust and the Council, now the tenants' management organisation (TMO) which manages all the housing originally owned and managed by the Council. In addition to these individual residents groups, there is the Colville Area Residents' Forum, which is an open forum that any local resident can attend.

Figure 2: Membership to Colville Area Council

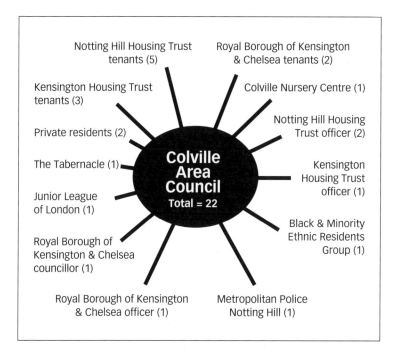

Finally there is the Colville Area Council. This is a carefully and democratically structured multi-agency group that brings together all the local stakeholders. The police send one representative. The tenants of Notting Hill Housing Trust, being the most numerous, have five representatives on the Council; Kensington Housing Trust tenants have three; TMO tenants have two, as do private residents. The Black and Minority Ethnic Residents Group has one representative. Tabernacle, the local community arts centre, has one representative. The Junior League of London, who have over the years made a substantially voluntary contribution, which

25

I will describe in Chapter five, has one representative. Colville Nursery has one representative. The representatives of the three social landlords are the final element of the Council.

Such a diverse group coming together in such a democratic structure is to be greatly welcomed. There are, however, some curious omissions – the local churches and primary schools. That should be remedied in the future. Close contact with Colville Primary School has been maintained over the past three years with the school's steel band playing at local events, a programme of energy efficiency training being run for pupils and the Colville Area Committee's AGM being held at the school. So their involvement in multi-agency structures, not just in local activities, should not be hard to bring about.

And in summary

108 has been integral to the success of the Colville Project. It has been a hub for the improvement works in the area, allowing residents access to the Colville project team and the facilities at 108. Most importantly, 108 is seen as a welcoming and comfortable space where people feel at ease to talk freely about whatever is on their mind. 108 has therefore been a source of knowledge and wisdom provided in an informal way, but by paid people, not by neighbours and local elders. It has been a semi-institutional alternative to what in the past would have happened informally through the generations of the community. At the beginning of this chapter, I said that people value constancy, familiarity and knowledge in the staff of the village shop. And that is what they have had with 108. But 108 has been engaged not in private trade but in public service.

Public service needs mutual aid in the community and selfless philanthropy from some of those who have. But it also needs public funds. And with public funds comes an obligation of accountability and an impetus for democracy. It will not do to say 'Give us the money. We're the local people. We know how to spend it.' Very many of the criticisms of public organisations - slow, bureaucratic - come in part from the need to be accountable. The success of 108 resides in combining accountability with effectiveness, accountability in public service with personal knowledge and familiarity. It is a rare combination, easily undervalued, often sought in vain and lost only at great peril.

And the need for neighbourhood democracy and accountability has never been greater. In the local government elections of 1998 turnout was 25 per cent in some London boroughs. In some wards, it was as low as 11 per cent. In Liverpool a council by-election, the outcome of which could change political control of the Council, attracted a turnout of six per cent. This was the culmination of much concern about the so-called 'democratic deficit'. Some feel that the disinterest in citizenship is a virus that brings multiple deprivation and social exclusion in its wake; not just an effect of deprivation, but a cause that twists the spiral downwards. So the whole nation needs new approaches to democratic renewal, not just for Wales and Scotland, and in the capital. At a highly local level too there is a need for new ideas for involvement. We need an updated form of parish councils, fit for our times. We need councils for urban villages. At least one of their functions would be to facilitate multi-agency working, an easy cause to espouse but one that has proved intransigent in its opposition to application in many places but not, I am pleased to report, at 108 Talbot Road.

Chapter three
The kingdom of individuals

"Under the surface of flux and fear there
is an underground movement
Under the crust of bureaucracy, quiet
behind the posters
Unconscious but palpably there - the
kingdom of individuals"

Louis MacNeice

For the first half of this century poor and working class people lived a good deal of their time in public spaces. Working class life had to be largely public because the private space was so inadequate. Even the housewife, still likely to be imprisoned behind four walls, shared in the public life of the market, in Portobello Road and neighbourhood parks. Young men and women met, danced and courted away from home. Men socialised in pubs, not called public for nothing, of which there were great numbers in the Colville area. Until the radio and then the cinema, which transformed the lives particularly of working class women, all forms of entertainment had to be in public, including, in the early years, watching television. From a football match to political meeting or holiday outing, life was experienced en masse.

The combination of a long post-war economic boom, full employment and the ready availability of cheaper versions of 'consumer' goods, previously only available to the rich such as cars and cameras as well as television and radio, have transformed the lives of working class people and that transformation continues. It is no longer even necessary to watch television or listen to music as a family. Many children and young adults have a TV and CD player in their rooms. Research by Sonia Livingstone at the London School of

Economics (reported in the *Guardian* on 4 March 1998) found that two thirds of British children now have a TV in their bedroom, double the number of other European children.

TV has made it unnecessary, even though still pleasurable, to go to a football match. Twenty eight million people watched England go out of the World Cup in 1998, losing a penalty shoot-out to Argentina. The vast majority watched it at home. Videos have made it unnecessary to go to the cinema. Perhaps most significant of all, telephones, now almost universally used, have made it possible to talk to friends and family without going out. It is not even necessary to live near people you talk to all the time. Finally cars, which two thirds of social housing tenants do not own, have meant, for those that have them, that visits can be made far and wide and still be home by evening. All have combined in a retreat to an expanded, secure private space.

These social changes have transformed the way that people see the domestic interior. From being an overcrowded barrack, a place of intrusion, coercion and sometimes violence to be escaped from at the first opportunity, it has become a kingdom of leisure, privacy and individuality – all things we have over recent years come to place an enormous value on. The consequence of this is inevitable. People ceased to find acceptable what the novelist Laurie Lee called "the honeyed squalor of home".

This profound re-configuring of family and social relationships, more complex than can be fully expounded here, can be expressed figuratively in this way:

The changing use of public and private space

Figure 3: Until the 1960s

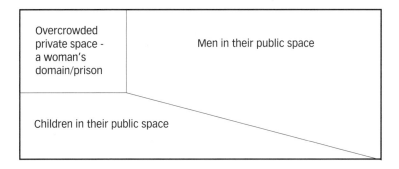

Figure 4: 1960s - 1990s

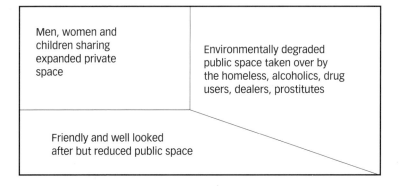

Figure 5: 1990s

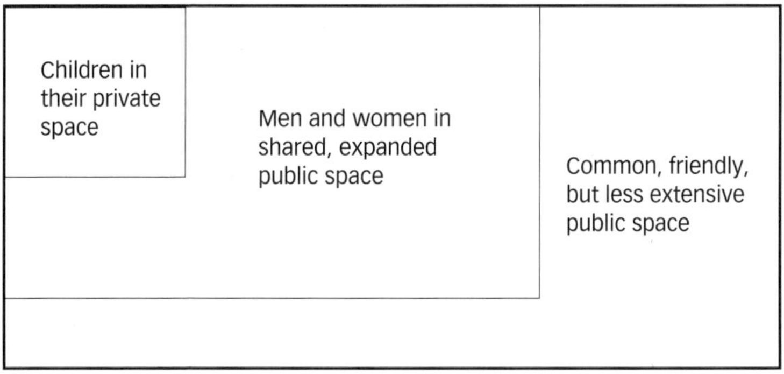

Over these years we moved from a society comprised largely of poor people to one in which there were vastly greater numbers of people who were comfortable and affluent. This period of post-war boom ended in the middle 1970s, but the full effects of its ending were not felt until the 1980s when the nostrums of the day were that business had to cut its costs, that is to say its people, and likewise shortly thereafter, the public sector too had to cut its costs and its people. And in cutting them, the quality of life in many urban neighbourhoods greatly deteriorated. But I am moving ahead too fast. We must first consider the impact of these changes in Colville and the new forces they uncorked which were, in the first instance, highly deleterious.

These changed aspirations finally brought recognition of the 'housing crisis' in the 1950s, which was as much the beginning of a 'crisis' of rising expectations, as a 'crisis' of decaying buildings. In 1957 well over a third of the houses were privately owned and much more of the population were privately renting. Much of it was squalid – more than a third lacked hot water and a fifth lacked exclusive use of a lavatory, but people had got used to low rents, much to the chagrin of Macmillan's government. The Housing Minister, the late Enoch Powell, introduced the 1957 Rent Act with a view to the controlled deregulation of rents in the belief that it would result in the feckless poor spending less money on drink and cigarettes and more on their rent. Landlords in their turn would spend more of their increased income on keeping properties in good repair. There would be an increase in moral behaviour all around. We do not know if he was right that less money got spent on decadent pleasure, but he was certainly wrong about the latter. As tenants moved out, rents could be reset free of controls, creating a huge financial incentive for landlords to coerce rent controlled tenants to move out, while doing little or nothing about much needed repairs.

Rachmanism

Perec Rachman, a Polish immigrant after the war, had started buying up the ends of leases of big multiply occupied houses in Notting Hill and other parts of West London. His methods of shifting tenants out of unfurnished rooms so that he could re-let them, nominally re-furnished and at vastly increased rents, have become the stuff of legend, not because his practices were so unusual but because he shared a prostitute with politicians who were catapulted into notoriety by the Profumo scandal, dragging him into an unwelcome limelight alongside them. Faced with a house full of statutory tenants paying protected rents, Rachman combined racial prejudice with business. According to the *Sunday Times*, he let one room to eight West Indians, 'all accomplished musicians', and told them he liked parties. Within three months 'the stats' – statutory tenants – left, replaced by ranks of West Indian immigrants or poor white people, desperate for housing and paying exorbitant rents amid appalling overcrowding. He owned 147 properties in West London involving at least 1,000 tenancies. Police gave these tenants little or no protection. Houses and flats in grave and worsening disrepair was one of the results. Jan O'Malley in her book, *The Politics of Community*, describes the resurgent role of housing trusts that had worked in the neighbourhood since the 1970s.

> "The Housing Crisis precipitated by the 1957 Rent Act restored the Trusts to the centre of the housing scene. The Council response was to give a loan of half a million pounds to Kensington Housing Trust on condition they agreed to take the 'fall-out' from the 1957 Housing Act, or in plain words – the casualties. Also the fresh sense of crisis created by the race riots, the scandals of Rachmanism and the persistent neglect of the Borough Council set the scene for the intervention of the Notting Hill Housing Trust in 1963."

Notting Hill Housing Trust

Reverend Bruce Kenrick and a group of volunteers established Notting Hill Housing Trust in 1963. They raised money to buy privately owned substandard properties, often with the aid of the Local Authority's planning powers. Once improved and converted into flats they were rented. In their first year they purchased five houses and housed 47 people; by 1966 they were purchasing three houses per month and by 1967 the number of homes in management stood at 288, including the Trust's first special needs housing project for ex-offenders and their families.

In 1972 the Colville Tavistock Study was undertaken by a Steering Group involving the Trust which reported on the needs and problems of the Colville area. The study recommended that 80-85 per cent of the housing stock in the area be bought into public ownership. The area was designated a Housing Action Area. The Council, Notting Hill Housing Trust and Kensington Housing Trust bought up, rehabilitated and redeveloped the remaining privately rented properties in the Colville area.

By the late 1990s Notting Hill Housing Trust has a portfolio of 3,000 properties in the borough of Kensington and Chelsea of which 550 dwellings are in the Colville area. Kensington Housing Trust owns 250 homes in the Colville area, the Local Authority 125 and the remainder are in the hands of private owners, both owner occupiers and some still owned by private landlords, who are now of a rather more benign variety than their antecedents in the 1950s and 1960s.

All this history means that many current social housing tenants arrived in the area more than 30 years ago, often members of black and white ethnic minorities, and having lived in squalid and overcrowded conditions when they first arrived. They came as tenants of private landlords. For some years now they have been tenants of social landlords, often in the same homes throughout. Their children are now adults, many still living with their parents and some working in the neighbourhood.

By 1992, 59 per cent of Notting Hill's properties had been converted at least 15 years previously. Of these almost half were converted before the more generous capital funding system of Housing Association Grant was brought in by the 1974 Housing Act. The acres of stucco which when painted lend a gay, colourful air to the neighbourhood, when peeling draw attention to decay. The extensive subsidence problems also meant that the costs of maintenance were high. Never having been converted to high standards, hundreds had sunk into considerable disrepair.

Apart from the rising expectations and the greater amount of time spent at home, alongside the disrepair, other problems too made the flats unpleasant places to live: the large rooms and windows made the cost of heating high. The heating systems and the standards of thermal insulation were inadequate. The sound proofing was poor and exacerbated by 'stacking' problems – families living in maisonettes above single people, sometimes single old people, thereby ensuring not only that children were likely to create an unacceptable level of noise, but also the children were denied the freer rein of the garden. Crime in the home was also a problem. Burglary, particularly of the poorly visible basement flats and through the weak front doors was a constant bane. To complete the catalogue, the means of escape in case of fire from many properties did not comply with current Building Regulations Standards.

All of this together with the degradation of the external environment and the problems of drugs and prostitution which will be discussed in the next chapter combined to produce an alarming statistic: 35.5 per cent of tenants said they wanted to move.

Reimproving homes

The reimprovement programme which was one of the primary objectives of the City Challenge endeavour after 1992, led to 'major works' on 127 properties, though had funds permitted, many more could have been, and needed to be, improved. Each improvement typically included repairs to the external fabric of the building, improvements to the internal layouts of the flats, renewal of mechanical and electrical services, new kitchen and bathroom fittings, installation of central heating, upgrading of thermal insulation, improved soundproofing and upgraded means of escape and security. In some properties new roofs, plumbing works and dry and wet rot treatment were also necessary. Extensive areas need replastering. Some flats were almost entirely rebuilt. In all £12.9 million was spent on improving housing, the area and building new homes between 1995 and 1998.

The true complexity of the task is hard to convey in words. The first and most difficult problem was where would the tenants go while the works were being done? Could the available housing owned by Notting Hill Housing Trust accommodate a major decanting programme? Probably not, so would it be possible to work around the tenants? A pilot project was carried out at 15/16 Powis Square, a large property containing 15 flats. It pretty quickly became clear that working around the tenants was a fraught option – the contracts were long and sometimes overran. The costs were high, higher than they would have been if the property had been empty. The disruption to the tenants' lives was enormous and they eventually tired of the 'battle', often after about six weeks of more or less constant disruption. The unexpected, in many forms, could be expected to make frequent appearances with consequences and upsets unforetold.

All of these problems were exacerbated by the introduction of new legislation – the Construction Design and Management regulations. These gave landlords greater responsibilities for the health and safety of tenants during the improvement works. While higher standards were welcome, the cost and logistics meant that this was the final straw. The decision was taken to decant tenants where major reimprovement works were to be done and not to continue the practice of working around tenants in situ.

A real risk then arose that empty properties could not be found for them to move into whilst works were being done, threatening to bring the entire repairs programme to a halt. With tenants awaiting decants jumping to the top of the transfer queue, all transfers on domestic or social grounds were postponed, greatly to the detriment of Trust tenants who were not directly benefiting from the reimprovement programme. The situation was unavoidable with the immediate need to take up available funds for improvements and to decant Colville tenants.

The sands of funding flowing through the quinquennial hourglass of City Challenge were in danger of stalling. Everything that could be done had to be done in five years. So there was a potential impasse here.

Housing Associations as Landlords

A solution was found in the 'Housing Associations as Landlords' scheme (HALS). Two houses in the Colville area containing 11 flats were rented from a private landlord and the whole population of several flats in another Notting Hill Housing Trust-owned house was moved together. The emptying of whole houses in this way was the quickest and most economic way of running the building contract, but it posed other problems. The disadvantage was that the commercial rents on the privately rented houses were high and the costs had to be borne by the Trust. Nonetheless it was an effective way of keeping the whole population 'churning' in a way that made it possible to make a huge and speedy impact on reimprovements and ensure that tenants could remain in the Colville area.

Some tenants did move out of the area by choice, mostly to the leafier suburbs to the west of North Kensington – Chiswick, Ealing and beyond to Hounslow. They were mostly people in their 40s and 50s with grown up children who may already have wanted to move away now that they had 'empty nests'.

So there are lessons to be learnt here for the future about undertaking a programme of reimprovement works:

• Don't underestimate the difficulties of working around tenants, especially in converted and scattered property.

• Be imaginative about decanting solutions. Otherwise you are in for a long hard search.

37

Tenant involvement and the Joint Improvement Group

One could hardly contemplate a major reimprovement programme without making a strong commitment to tenant involvement. But like so many indisputably good ideas, this commitment is easier to enunciate than to enact. In the early days of the Colville Project it was envisaged that tenants would be consulted individually about the options and decisions available for their homes as well as being asked for their views in groups. In order to arrive at redesign solutions for whole houses, it became clear that all residents had to be consulted together. Not only did individual decisions affect everyone, but group pressure was sometimes needed to achieve a consensus. Dealing with tenants one to one often did not work well either for them or for Notting Hill Housing Trust. House meetings were an important step with tenants meeting their neighbours for the first time, which often resulted in friendships being forged and mutual support being offered. In one house two tenants agreed to swap flats so that the tenant with 'poor legs' could live on a lower floor. Tenants in another house in Powis Square redesigned the communal area for bikes and pushchairs and created a communal entrance and 'house' garden.

Their residents association was one forum in which tenants could become involved as a group. The Joint Improvement Group was another. The appealing acronym, JIG, was given to a group including representatives from the tenants' association for Notting Hill tenants in the Colville area (CPTAG), Notting Hill Housing Trust and staff from the Colville Project.

JIG was a great success. The group initiated many changes in approaches to reimprovements and brought about new initiatives including the tenants' information handbook, 'Major Improvements to Your Home'. This contained contact names and telephone numbers, information on moving temporarily for works and on the availability of compensation. JIG was also instrumental in defining a framework of choices for tenants. A strong feeling grew that too open-ended a choice for tenants was logistically complex for the staff and could lead to inequitable distribution of limited largesse, as well as raising tenants' expectations to unachievable heights.

Striking the right balance between the responsibilities of the landlord and the obligations of the tenant is not straightforward. So one tenant I met felt that it was the landlords' responsibility to see that pigeons did not collect on the roof or windowsills of her home. Another wanted a leaking tap fixed. What would they have done if they were owner occupiers? Presumably the pigeons would have been frightened off once and for all in ways that only human ingenuity can devise, or she would put up with it. The leaking tap would have been fixed or carried on leaking. So where or why does the landlord come in?

On the other hand, I was told of examples of people being recharged or refused permission to alter their homes to their own taste because some imaginary future tenant would not like what they wanted to do. When they pointed out that they had no intention of moving, so the situation feared was not going to arise, they were still denied permission. This seems perverse and bureaucratic. I was told of one tenant who had painted her flat on moving and then having the cost of repainting it deducted from her Tenants Incentive Scheme allocation when she moved out, which seems unreasonably punitive. Social landlords seem to have got themselves into an invidious position, simultaneously giving too much and too little choice.

So what are the legitimate boundaries between tenant involvement, customer care and the tenants' own responsibilities? Do all the stakeholders have a shared view? Often different departments of the same organisation cannot agree, let alone the tenants. This has all become rather irrational and is long overdue for a major overhaul. Perhaps it always was. It's just that landlords did not notice. The tenants certainly did. A forum such as JIG helps to iron out these inconsistencies, share information and create a space for difficulties experienced by groups or individuals to be addressed.

Tenant Liaison Officer

Because of some of the problems just described, in the second year it became clear that more consistent and continuous personal contact was needed between the tenants whose homes were being reimproved and the contractors, consultants and landlord. Too many people and organisations were involved, exponentially increasing the likelihood of mistakes and misunderstandings. The scale of the programme had also increased. JIG concluded that a Tenant Liaison Officer based at 108 was needed. Her demanding job was to seek to give the tenants what they wanted, within the bounds of what the landlord would permit and could afford. The job of establishing and managing the difficult balance described above fell to her. She also had to provide ongoing advice and information to the tenants through the period of reimprovement. Getting the works going was the easy bit once contract negotiations and decanting arrangements had been put in place to reassure tenants; the capacity for confusion grew ever greater from that moment on. Having a dedicated member of staff who could hold dilemmas, conflicts and things not quite going according to plan in one place and pass information on to all those who needed it was a great benefit. But it needed a clear structure. Leaving things too open-ended is a sure way to raise and then to dash expectations.

So once the Tenant Liaison Officer was in place, the planned programme of house meetings, discussions with individual tenants and consultations on site could begin and meetings of the JIG could be co-ordinated by one person. She could also establish and communicate a transparent and fair framework for tenants' choices. Because the best laid plans of mice and men are more likely to go wrong in a building contract than in almost any other circumstances, when problems did occur she could work through the difficulties with the tenants. Once the work was complete, the tenants received a handover pack about their new-old home from the Tenant Liaison Officer. She dealt with any defects that arose shortly after the completion of the contract and gave advice on energy efficiency. Finally she dealt with claims for compensation if there were any.

So there are important lessons to be learnt for the future here:

- Clearly define and state the parameters of tenant choice and involvement in the reimprovement of their home and indeed in all other tenancy matters.

- A named individual needs to manage the relationship between the tenants and everyone else involved in the reimprovement. Without a one-stop contact, muddle and disappointment will surely ensue.

- Liaison is needed throughout the contract until the completion of the defects period, not just while it's being planned.

- A forum for setting consistent standards and dealing with any difficulties may also be needed.

There is one final lesson to be learnt from the reimprovement programme: many tenants told us that the process of coming together with their neighbours to talk through the improvements had the most desirable consequence of strengthening relationships between them. They may have lived near or by each other for years, but in many instances had barely exchanged even superficial civilities. People need a reason to get to know one another, particularly in the urban context and particularly in Britain. Most commonly, of course, people who live near each other get to know one another not through being neighbours, but through their children attending the same school. I will discuss this at greater length in Chapter five. The reimprovement works were also an important nexus around which people got to know each other better.

Home security

In 1992, 59 per cent of Kensington Housing Trust tenants felt unsafe in their own homes. On average 72 burglaries took place each year in the neighbourhood between 1990 and 1992. The British Crime Survey has found that having neighbours who have been burgled is a good predictor of people being concerned about burglary, whereas knowing people from outside the area who have been burgled did not increase levels of worry. This suggests that perceptions of risk are very place specific: the risks of burglary run by those friends and relatives who live outside one's immediate area are not taken into account when calculating one's own risk. So such a high incidence of burglary in such a small neighbourhood certainly greatly increased local people's fears, as many of them told us.

The use of porches, steps, basements and other secluded common areas for prostitution and drug dealing by people who were not tenants or even local residents was a serious and sometimes frightening nuisance. In 1990/1 a security scheme was funded by the Urban Programme as a joint initiative between the Royal Borough of Kensington and Chelsea Environmental Health Department and the Notting Hill Police to carry out security improvements in the area. Brendan Brett, Crime Prevention Officer, recognised that it was not just individual homes that needed their security improved. "The homes which received security were deemed the most urgent at the time, but it was also realised that the whole area required a survey and security upgrade to restore confidence and improve the quality of life for the residents".

Close liaison with Notting Hill Police's Crime Prevention Officer was the linchpin of the scheme. Residents were offered a security survey, with properties that had been burgled given priority. The staff at 108 Talbot Road referred others, who had not heard about them, to the Crime Prevention Officer for security surveys. Once the surveys were completed, staff at the Colville project identified possible sources of funding for the security improvement works, often from the Colville Project's City Challenge funds.

City Challenge money was targeted at bringing low-cost security measures to the maximum number of dwellings by the Colville Project. The project also worked closely with the Police to identify those houses most vulnerable and in need of improvements.

As part of a separate campaign 70 basements were secured. One hundred and seventy-three properties were made more secure as part of major works schemes. One hundred and ninety-two cowls were fitted to letterboxes, 92 porch lights were fitted and two community premises were secured. And did it work? In 1997 there were 44 burglaries in the Colville area, a reduction from the average of 72 a year already mentioned.

An important lesson can be learnt from this experience:

• Funding is not always available at the beginning of a new campaign or initiative. We shall see this pattern again and again. The need for action is identified. The extent of the need is then uncovered and then funds are sought and found. The process is not opportunistic. It is responsive. It is not that ideas and innovations follow money, but that money is found for good ideas identified by local residents, and then co-ordinated by community development workers.

Energy efficiency

Less than half the world's population lives in cities. But they are consuming three quarters of the world's energy and causing at least three-quarters of global pollution. Worse still, cities have giant ecological footprints – an area scattered throughout the world and vastly greater than the physical boundary of the city itself on which the city depends. These footprints supply the resources and provide sites for the disposal of waste. We have, for the first time in human history, reached a kind of Armageddon. The ecological footprints of existing cities now cover the entire globe. Richard Rogers, the architect and city planner, comments in his book on sustainable cities, *Cities for a Small Planet,*

"The expansion of urban ecological footprints is taking place simultaneously with the erosion of fertile lands, living seas and virgin rain forests. Given this simple supply constraint, urban ecological footprints must be dramatically reduced and circumscribed."

Agenda 21, the plan that emerged from the 'Earth Summit' in Rio de Janeiro in June 1992, laid great stress on managing and reducing consumption as a way of preventing these footprints reaching even more gigantic proportions.

> "The major cause of global environmental deterioration is an unsustainable pattern of consumption and production, particularly in the industrialised countries, which aggravates poverty and imbalances...To encourage greater efficiency in the use of energy and resources, governments should reduce the amount of energy and materials per unit in the production of goods and services, promote the dissemination of existing environmentally sound technologies, promote research and development in environmentally sound technologies."

We have already talked in the first part of this book of globalisation. The global ecological footprints of cities is a most unwelcome form of globalisation. Small local actions to reverse these disturbing trends, taken together, will count for much. A great difference could be made as the Government has recognised in passing the Home Energy Conservation Act in 1996. And such action has been taken in the last five years in Colville.

Tenants wanted to heat their homes affordably, to maintain comfortable temperatures, to reduce condensation problems and of course to pay less in fuel bills. The landlords too had reasons to invest in energy efficiency. They wanted to provide a healthier environment for their tenants, keep their buildings in better condition and to reduce complaints from their tenants. They also recognised that reducing fuel poverty might make it easier for the tenants to pay their rent and so have a beneficial impact on the ever-present problem of rent arrears.

Notting Hill Housing Trust improved the energy efficiency of 96 of their properties – thermally dry lining walls, installing double glazed windows when new ones were installed. Windows and doors were draught proofed. More efficient boilers and heating systems were installed. Lighting could also be made more energy efficient, and time switches in communal areas also reduced energy consumption. Insulation to roofs, basements and at the ends of terraces was increased.

Here is another lesson with wide repercussions:

- I have said that 96 of Notting Hill's properties were made more energy efficient, as well as the 127 that received major reimprovements, which automatically included energy packages. Others needed the improvements too. But time and money ran out. Much good was done during the five years of City Challenge, but the moment at which it ended seems almost arbitrary. This applies to the energy efficiency works and to many other subjects besides. The time limits seem arbitrary and hard to justify.

The *Commission on Social Justice* observed in 1994 about City Challenge and other similar regeneration initiatives:

"The common denominator is the short-term approach to regeneration: problems which have taken decades to develop cannot be solved quickly, and certainly not according to the vagaries of the electoral cycle. It takes political guts to invest in projects whose dividends will only be reaped beyond the term of a parliament or a council cycle; but it is necessary none the less."

Many hearts in North Kensington will return an echo to these sentiments, particularly amongst those whose homes have yet to be improved.

Pinehurst Court

The energy efficiency campaign like most of the work done by the Colville Project went beyond social housing. In January 1996 an article was placed in the bulletin inviting residents with heating problems to contact the Colville Project. Eighty per cent of those who responded were from a privately owned block of flats. Originally nine separate five storey houses, they had been laterally converted into 105 flats, collectively renamed Pinehurst Court. Without a gas supply, there was no central heating in the flats. Many of the flats were small and the people living in them could afford to do little to improve them.

Having received these responses and recognised a general not an individual problem, the Colville Project asked to meet members of the residents' committee of Pinehurst Court. Following the meeting a survey was carried out. The residents had the common problem of large, draughty windows in small flats. In addition, many of the storage heaters were obsolete and the roof insulation was either poor or non-existent.

The Colville Project appointed the Energy Audit Company to assess the energy efficiency of the block and to recommend low-cost energy efficient measures. The Colville Project also brought in London Electricity to advise. They had half an eye on the possibility that London Electricity might provide funding. Working with the residents and these organisations, a range of energy improvements were offered: overhauling the windows; water cylinder jackets; water heater time clocks; draught stripping and energy efficient light bulbs. Those residents who were not on benefit contributed 50 per cent of the cost. The balance was funded by grants from London Electricity and City Challenge. A third of the flats benefited from these improvements. Also, roof insulation was put in for the whole block.

Energy information

A feature of many interventions by social landlords is that they make the physical improvements, involving the residents to the extent that is necessary to do the work to homes and then leave the residents, hopefully, to enjoy gratefully the benefits bestowed on them. Life is always more complex. A survey of residents in social housing in the neighbourhood with new central heating systems showed that, although 93 per cent were satisfied with their energy improvements, only 12 per cent reported a reduction in fuel bills. Apparently they did not fully understand how their heating system controls worked and had not reduced their energy consumption as envisaged. One of the key objectives of the considerable investment had in large measure failed.

In response on Monday 22 April 1996 the Colville Energy Information Day was held at the Tabernacle, the local community arts centre. Despite a relatively small turnout of residents, new contacts and partnerships were forged with other organisations operating on the energy efficiency beat, including Royal Borough of Kensington and Chelsea Project Control, British Gas, London Electricity and the Tenants' Energy Advisory Service. These organisations came together to develop an energy strategy for the Colville Project. That in turn led to a pilot project between the Colville Project and the Royal Borough of Kensington and Chelsea – the Colville Winter Energy Campaign, funded by the Department of the Environment, which had been given the power and resources to do this as a result of the passage of the Home Energy Conservation Act.

The Home Energy Conservation Act (HECA) came into force in April 1996. It required local authorities to find measures by which a 30 per cent reduction in CO_2 emissions can be made in areas of residential accommodation over the next 10 years. This followed the Earth Summit in Rio de Janeiro and growing international concern about the ecological footprints left by cities that have already been described.

Because Colville is a multi-tenure neighbourhood with an already established infrastructure for working with and for local people, it was the perfect place for a pilot that might, in due course, be extended to the rest of the borough. The Colville Project received funding of £60,000 to address the issues of energy conservation and awareness. In November 1996, a Colville Energy Advice Worker was appointed to lead the six-month home energy project.

The campaign aimed to reduce energy consumption in domestic properties, to lower fuel bills and to increase thermal comfort. The methods to be deployed were training, grants information and advice. Some of the achievements of the campaign are listed:

- One hundred staff from 12 voluntary, private and public sector organisations took part in energy training and seminar sessions.

- Twenty two front line staff achieved City & Guilds qualifications in Energy Awareness.

- Eight hundred hours of front line staff time was committed to the campaign.

- One hundred residents attended the Energy Advice Week held in May 1997.

- Eleven local representatives attended an Energy Awareness Course.

- Two hundred thousand pounds was taken up in energy grants predominantly by Notting Hill tenants but also by the wider community.

- Two hundred and fifty Notting Hill Housing Trust properties were identified to take up grants.

After the initial six-month pilot the energy efficiency project continued with other initiatives. The Colville Energy Advisor has undertaken energy audits on community premises and blocks of sheltered flats for older people. He also initiated a schools energy awareness programme involving parents and children at Colville Primary School.

So far, so good. A very high proportion of local residents received home improvements of some kind over the five year period. This ranged from those 100 people who received free low energy lightbulbs and those whose homes were installed with security letter boxes, to many others who benefited from substantial home improvements. Making private space more pleasant and affordable to live in supports the aspirations that have grown in people's minds in recent decades to have an aesthetically pleasing, individually styled, comfortable place to call home. It has been part of the growing wealth of the nation and much welcomed by most people, here in Colville and elsewhere. Reimproving their property could be seen as social landlords securing their investment. From the tenants' point of view, it is more likely to be seen as a belated move to the spirit of modern times.

Next I turn our attention to the public space. Much needed to be done to bring this to the standards of contemporary expectations too.

Chapter four
In the public space

"The long tradition of the village green, the market square, the public commons, lammas lands, the town square and the Victorian park have all been central to a sense of local identity and belonging. This line of innovation and renewal now seems exhausted in many places. What will this generation leave future generations in the way of exciting, diverse, rich and sustainable places in our towns and cities, places where they will find a sense of continuity, of relief from the pressures of urban living, places to be in touch with the natural cycles of the seasons, and of wildlife, and also places both to be alone at times but also places to meet and celebrate with others?"

Park Life: Urban parks and social renewal, Comedia and Demos

Open spaces in the city fulfil many complex urban needs. People who use them, use them frequently; usually they walk to them. People of all ages and from all walks of life use them to take children out, to walk the dog, to look on something beautiful, to meet someone and talk, to get out of the house, to be alone with your thoughts for a while or just to take the air.

People see parks and public spaces as the places where memories are made; where they mark the passing stages of their lives. There they played their early childhood games. Maybe it was also the stage set of the drama of adolescent rebellion, perhaps even vandalism and destruction. But it is also where they might have gone courting, and then had their wedding photographs taken. Once they had children of their own they would take them to the park to play. Later on they would take their grandchildren and finally, they might mark the loss of a loved one with an inscribed park bench.

And there are other functions too. For some people, conversations in public spaces are more intimate than those at home. Sitting on the bench for hours talking can be like going to confession, or seeking counselling. And, on the other hand, people go and sit in the square to read, or write, or reflect - to engage in private, solitary activity in a public, convivial place, bringing together the individual and the collective.

But all of this requires that the squares and park are attractive, well-maintained and that they feel safe. And this had become far from the case. The declining qualities of Britain's urban parks and open spaces is now a matter of grave public concern. It is part of a wider fear that we can no longer manage safety and well-being in public spaces. The 'keeper-less' park along with the unstaffed railway station, the poorly lit underground car park, the unsupervised playground and the deserted town centre at night are all close to becoming endemic features of our urban environment. JK Galbraith was the first to capture in the public mind the mismatch between private affluence and public squalor which had reached alarming proportions by the middle 1980s. In the 1984 introduction to his seminal study of the changes in the post-war economy, *The Affluent Society*, he notes:

> "In a typical urban community today the citizen leaves his comfortable apartment or house with all of its internal manifestations of affluence to wade through filth, wondering all the while if the next block or passage shields someone with a design on his person or pocketbook."

The urban village had lost some of the most important qualities of village life - safe and familiar streets and open spaces where you might meet those that you already know. Those that you do not know would not be a threat. The Colville area had become almost a cliché by the early 1990s – disfigured public open spaces and crime openly and frequently committed on the streets. If regeneration was to mean anything at all the open spaces had to be improved, local people had to be more involved in looking after their local environment and crime had to be cleared from the streets.

The Colville neighbourhood

By 1992 the grand houses laid out around elegant green town squares - Colville and Powis - had become peeling cliffs of shabby stucco surrounding a degraded environment, brown not green, poor or no play equipment, benches used by the winos and junkies, avoiding if they could enormous amounts of evenly-dispersed dog shit and piles of rubbish. Flimsy carrier bags, caught by the wind, hung from trees like ugly flowers. A supermarket trolley, its wheels wonkier than ever, stood monumentally in the square, almost as if someone would be back for it shortly. But they never returned. Graffiti was an infectious rash. At the centre of Colville Square was Colville Nursery's enclosed play area. Parents and teachers felt most uncomfortable about its use by small children. These spaces were neither green, pleasant nor public anymore.

'Winos', referred to locally as 'the drinking school', sat like sentries at the entrance to Colville Square, defecating, if need be, in the gardens and abusing passers by who were doing their best to pass unnoticed and uncommented upon. For all practical purposes the square was a no-go area for all but the most determined of dog walkers. As one local resident desperately observed, "The public will not walk through the square due to the disgusting activities occurring."

Even so, the various schemes and plans put forward for 'designing out' this and other forms of anti-social behaviour elicited a concerned response. Some local people were, for moral and political reasons, reluctant to see the socially excluded excluded from the square. They feared also that they would simply be displaced elsewhere.

Powis Square was once private 25 years ago. As a result of campaigning and demonstrations which culminated in residents tearing down the fences and 'liberating' the square, it was brought into public use in 1977. Colville Square had also been private and had been compulsorily purchased by the Council. Of all the many town squares in the Royal Borough of Kensington and Chelsea, these are the only two that have been brought into public use. For these reasons and because 75 per cent of households in the neighbourhood have

53

no private gardens, the condition of these squares, freedom of access to them and the pleasure to be derived from using them are all dear to the hearts of local people. So they were an important priority in the regeneration of the neighbourhood.

Community Land and Workspace Services Ltd (CLAWS) were commissioned to undertake an independent consultation exercise about the squares. Their survey was made in June 1993 in the earliest days of the Colville Project. Two hundred and forty six residents were interviewed. Even more became involved in open days. The report produced set the following priorities for local residents:

- A safe play area for under 13s.

- A generally cleaner, safer environment.

- A greener space.

- Combating anti-social behaviour.

Seventy-seven per cent of people were also concerned about dogs fouling; 66 per cent were concerned about litter; 54 per cent were concerned about anti-social behaviour; 45 per cent wanted quiet sitting areas; 43 per cent noted the lack of investment; 35 per cent felt unsafe and 34 per cent complained about poor maintenance.

Colville Square

After some consultation, the Parks Department of the Council proposed the final scheme which local residents had designed. The project was managed by the Council. The works were funded by City Challenge and Notting Hill Housing Trust. The design of the square was developed particularly with young children and older people in mind reflecting the priorities identified by CLAWS. These two groups were the people most likely to use and derive the greatest benefit from using public open space. So a quiet, floral garden was established, as well as improved facilities for children under the age of five. The improvements were also meant to design out crime. High shrubbery was removed to improve the sight lines across the square. Hiding places were removed, as were benches.

But the works to Colville Square did not go wholly to plan. They were protracted with no timescale agreed in advance and implementing the plan took over three years. Plans were not carried out as originally proposed and residents felt their opinions were not truly heard and acted upon. Some felt, and still feel, that the landscaping was basic and unimaginative in order to facilitate low cost and irregular council maintenance, rather than to give pleasure to local people. The planting was still not fully established in 1998. The arches, intended to be covered with roses, were still bare wood and the garden had yet to mature.

Nevertheless, once the works were complete, most local residents regarded them as a success on balance. The gardens did not have the plants that most of the residents wanted and the quality of the works was not everything that could have been wished for but, as one local resident said, "We wanted to get rid of the winos and junkies and give our children a safe place to play in – we did that and that was our greatest effect."

Colville Alley

Colville Alley, a strip of no man's land between Colville Square and the adjacent high-sided houses, also felt unsafe and degraded. It became a magnet for rubbish dumping. Drug users saw a good secluded place to hide and continued their habit in relative peace. In order to overcome these problems, part of the alley was adopted by the Council and included in Colville Square. The other part of it was incorporated into individual gardens. Walls were extended, gardens separated and security fences were installed at the end of the gardens. An added benefit was that Hammersmith College, which many local people attend, carried out the works.

Powis Square

Having learnt from the experience of improving Colville Square, local residents wanted a greater say not only in what improvements were made, but also the process by which they were to be made in neighbouring Powis Square. Ways of gaining greater control were identified by local people. The appointment of an independent landscape architect was suggested, a wish City Challenge was reluctant to accede to. However a fuller consultation exercise was undertaken. It was not intended to be quite as full as it turned out to be. It was originally scheduled to last three months. In fact it took six. The range of users and uses, and the many shades of opinion expressed, made it sometimes feel that no agreement would ever be reached.

The most divisive issue was dogs. Opinion divided between those who thought that dogs had a right to roam, and to poo, and those who had children, who felt that their children's right to roam was severely compromised by dog owners who did not clear up after their dog. As the byelaws stood, dog owners could use the square and the best efforts of their opponents proved insufficient to change that. The dog owners of the neighbourhood got themselves well-organised into the Powis Pets and Friends Association and showed that community organisations can be brought to the aid of all kinds of causes for which there is sufficient local support, showing there is no universal consensus. Debates grew more and more heated. The final public meeting attended by more than 70 people overheated and had to be brought to a premature close. Notwithstanding the strong opinions expressed, many felt that the meeting had been a success! The community in all its diversity, strength and character had had its say.

The works finally agreed were complementary to those undertaken in Colville Square. Those sections of the community who benefited from Colville were not given top priority in Powis Square. The equipment installed in Powis Square was intended for use by children over five. So a climbing frame was built funded by a voluntary group, the Junior League of London, whose contribution to the neighbourhood. I will discuss in the next chapter. There were two play areas and a pitch marked out for basketball and football and many new trees. The result was an upgrade of what had been there before. A more radical solution would have required an architect more skilled at getting groups of people away from the lowest common denominator and towards a more creative and imaginative consensus than in fact was achieved.

Once more the works took longer than anticipated. The standard was also not all that had been wished for. Nonetheless, the works were greatly welcomed, particularly the facilities for children. The Council remains reluctant to bring in byelaws insisting that dog owners 'scoop the poop' and keep dogs on a lead, though they have begun. Their worry is that byelaws are worthless without staff to enforce them and of these there are few.

Many lessons can be learnt from the experience of planning and undertaking these works:

• Be realistic about the length of time environmental improvement works are going to take.

• Don't offer to consult people unless you intend to listen to their suggestion. If there are limits to what can be afforded or achieved, set out those limits at the beginning of the process.

• Focus on the needs of children and old people. If they are satisfied, adults, particularly working adults, are also likely to be satisfied. The latter after all use community facilities far less.

• Appoint a landscape architect experienced at working with the community.

• Define responsibilities, commitments and boundaries between local agencies clearly at an early stage.

The Canyon

Colville Gardens, with high stucco-ed houses on both sides, is known locally as the Canyon. On one side of the street the houses, Pinehurst Court, the private block of flats mentioned in the last chapter, had in the early 1970s reversed their aspect and decided to look out over their original rear gardens. So one side of the Canyon is the indifferent rear aspects. On the other side of the street the houses had over the years lost their porches, detailed cornices and architraves. They had become huge, flat-fronted cliffs. The street is wide and had become a rat run for traffic from Westbourne Park Road via Clydesdale Road through to Westbourne Grove. The junctions at both ends were dangerous. The possibility of an accident was never far away. The nickname 'the Canyon' reflected the feel of this desolate, steep-sided, windy causeway. Residents were fed up with rubbish dumped everyday on the street, with nowhere to store it once Environmental Health had condemned the basement refuse stores. The broken bags were only to the taste of locally resident rats, which were plentiful.

By July 1995, residents had become exasperated and exhausted by the whole ugly scene. They also saw that many other areas in the neighbourhood were being improved, giving them a sense of possibility. They compiled a petition setting out the problems of the street and lobbied City Challenge, local councillors and the housing associations. The Colville Project took up their cause and arranged a meeting with them and the Council's Chair of Environmental Services. An imaginative way forward was found. An architectural competition between six local architects was initiated to obtain proposals for the street. At the exhibition of the proposals residents and local workers voted for their preferred options. A steering group of senior staff from the housing associations, the Council, councillors and tenants' representatives made the final choice of scheme.

Then the funds had to be found. Tenants firstly lobbied City Challenge who agreed to provide £100,000 which was matched by £100,000 in charitable funds from Notting Hill

Housing Trust. To find the additional £250,000 the Colville Project approached the London Borough of Kensington and Chelsea's Highways Department who also agreed to put up a further £100,000. The Council's Housing Department agreed to make a contribution of £60,000 to cover their three properties and an additional payment of £38,500 was made from City Challenge to cover lighting and trees, once the scheme had been completed and was seen to be a success.

Again we see the same pattern which I identified in the last chapter - funds are found once a need has been identified and solutions devised. Established networks in the community were called upon during this set of complicated negotiations with the agencies involved. It is a community-led and people-centred process. It is not led by funders.

The project managers of the work were staff at the Colville Project. New porches were put on the front of the houses. The porches ingeniously incorporated concealed spaces in which to store rubbish. The lower halves of the houses were painted sunshine yellow to brighten a street of long dark shadows. A complete repaint would have been preferable but was too costly. Trees were planted along the road to diminish the bleakness of the aspect. The road was narrowed and the pavements were widened. The traffic was calmed with speed humps. New lighting was installed, both on the street and in the porches. The scheme was completed on time and residents expressed great satisfaction.

All Saints Piazza

The pedestrinanised area in front of All Saints Church, known locally as the Piazza, prevents the traffic from driving straight down Talbot Road. Prostitutes had developed the habit of leaving the phone numbers of the telephone boxes in All Saints Piazza on cards stuck in other telephone boxes around Bayswater and Paddington. So punters rang the phones in the Piazza and the prostitutes awaited their calls. Sometimes the prostitutes were not there, but the punters still called and the phones rang and rang, much to the irritation of local people. Drug dealing too had reached epidemic proportions, often conducted behind large shrubs in planters, handily designed and placed for use as post boxes for messages to drug dealers. The planters also provided easy concealment and therefore engendered maximum fear in passers-by not in the market for drugs or prostitutes just now; just, in fact, on their way to purchase the more humdrum produce available in Portobello Road market, but having to 'run the gauntlet' first. In order to make the future brighter for local residents, drug dealers and prostitutes were going to have to be made to migrate.

The huge brick planting tubs were removed and replaced with new trees planted in the pavement in an avenue. A passer-by can now see all the way down Talbot Road from Ledbury Road to Portobello Road without trees or planting tubs obscuring the view. The telephone boxes were also removed. A cycle path was integrated across the Piazza to create a throughflow of people.

The improvements to the Piazza have been an unqualified success. The church is now beautifully floodlit, pouring a gentle light across the Piazza at night. People walk up and down Talbot Road across the Piazza without fear of encountering anti-social or terrifying behaviour. Cyclists can pass through and children can play without their parents worrying about the cars, which are still prevented from crossing the Piazza.

Neighbourhood environmental initiatives

Apart from these major environmental improvements, a number of smaller initiatives have contributed to the improvement of the quality of the environment in the neighbourhood, and thereby to the quality of life.

Adopt a Tree

A key question about all environmental improvements is sustainability. Local residents repeatedly asked the Council to provide a park keeper for the two squares and wanted to be involved in planting, but without success. How can one ensure that, once improvements have been made, people feel sufficiently responsible for them to prevent them becoming neglected, abused and degraded? Once 27 trees had been planted in the Canyon, a scheme was initiated to 'Adopt a Tree'. The imaginative idea was that local residents should, if they volunteered, take responsibility for the wellbeing of one tree. All were adopted and both the trees and their carers will hopefully develop a sense of belonging. Unlike the trees in the squares, which were not adopted, these have thrived with the tender loving care of their adoptive owners.

But only asking people to adopt a tree was overly cautious. Strong feelings had been expressed about the quality of the landscaping of Powis Square and Colville Square. Negative views had been expressed about the management of the improvement works by the Council's Parks Department. Surely the local residents could have been asked to look after the open space. There are plenty of examples around the country of residents associations managing communal gardens. It would only have been one small idealistic step further to suggest that a residents' group might have landscaped and looked after the public open spaces, perhaps with some financial help from the Council.

One thing is for certain: if local residents had been given responsibility for looking after the park, the conflict over the dogs would have been resolved. Residents who allowed their dogs to foul the squares would have been challenged by other watchful local residents who were involved with maintaining the squares. I am not seeking to encourage busybodies, but to create self-regulating arrangements within the community. It is, in the end, impossible for local authorities or landlords to regulate the behaviour of their tenants and other residents when their staff are not present most of the time, even though byelaws have finally been passed insisting on 'poop being scooped.' A collective agreement within the community is needed and a common will to enforce it. A custom of good behaviour is necessary, rather than seeking to penalise bad behaviour with ineffectual laws which are difficult to police. Customs are always more powerful than laws. There is some evidence to support the proposition that local residents would be willing to make a voluntary contribution to maintaining the local environment as I have been suggesting.

Keep Colville Tidy

The 'Keep Colville Tidy' campaign was launched with the Colville Tidy Day on 29th September 1996. Organised with the Junior League of London, about whom more will be said in the next chapter, 50 people spent the day giving the area a facelift – cleaning off graffiti and fly posters, sweeping the streets and washing down play equipment.

The campaign took other initiatives too, such as mail-outs to all households and posters displayed locally giving information about rubbish and recycling collections. Environment problem cards were given to residents to report problems in their own street.

Blooming Balconies

Even with these improvements, green spaces and flowers are hard to find in North Kensington. So the residents of Kensington Housing Trust organised a 'Blooming Balconies' competition. Working with the staff of the 108, the residents raised funds, both for prizes and to encourage those who did not have any plants to try again next year. But the residents did not feel that their fingers were green enough. In response, the Junior League organised a workshop on creating and maintaining window boxes. Over 30 people attended and the workshop was a great success. The results can be seen all over the Colville area. The Blooming Balconies project will be run again.

Adopt a Tree, Keep Colville Tidy and Blooming Balconies are all examples of mutual aid and I will discuss others in the next chapter. They are examples of voluntary activity for common benefit, which engage people with one another and, over time, create emotional and practical mutual obligations to their neighbours and their neighbourhood. The underlying ethos of City Challenge as I said in the first chapter was to "inspire the community with the self-confidence to realise its underlying potential". Inspiration comes more from the things that people do together than it does from all the expensive capital projects in the world. So the importance of small activities which involve large numbers of people should never be diminished. They are the lifeblood of community; the foundation for sustainable community involvement. Our rich tradition of voluntary organisations in Britain is testimony to that. The anthropologist Margaret Mead put it well, "Never doubt that a small group of thoughtful, committed citizens can change the world: indeed, it's the only thing that ever does."

Drugs and crime

Even if the physical environment is improved, the activities taking place can be a source of great disquiet to local people. And as I have said, there was much going on to make one uncomfortable on the streets and in the public spaces of Colville - prostitution in All Saints Piazza, junkies and winos in Colville and Powis Squares and drug users in Colville Alley. Jane Jacobs noted in her classic book, *The Death and Life of Great American Cities*, "The bedrock attribute of a successful city is that a person must feel personally safe and secure amongst all these strangers." And this attribute was conspicuous by its absence.

Perhaps the most visible evidence of the malaise over the neighbourhood was the drug problems. Soft and hard drugs were dealt quite openly on the streets. Drugs were also taken on the street. Users, visibly disoriented by crack, the more pernicious and cheaper variant of cocaine, were to be seen in the streets, or in dark corners, in alleys, in basements and behind shrubs. One resident told of the shock of opening the curtains to the front window of her basement flat to be confronted by two people shooting up heroin about six inches away on the other side of the pane of the glass.

Some dealers and users had once been local residents, or were known to, or related to local residents. One of the features of drug abuse is that it puts drug users beyond the reach of their families and communities, even if old friends and relatives are quite nearby. Determination to squander all available resources, their own and other people's, on drugs, and the anti-social and unpredictable behaviour that invariably attends hard drug use, means that friends and family members can only take so much. Serious drug users fall back on the company of those who share their obsession.

This rift between local people and drug users meant there was little sympathy for the activities taking place, but the means of tackling the problem were not agreed upon. Using CCTV cameras to gather evidence about criminal activity was hotly debated. Some local people opposed the use of CCTV at meetings of the Colville Area Council. They felt that it was an abuse of civil liberties. Others felt that it would simply displace the problem. The Colville Area Council as a whole remained neutral. An independent survey of local residents commissioned by City Challenge showed that there was majority support for the installation of the cameras. CCTV was installed throughout North Kensington in July 1997, though the opponents won some important safeguards.

In the event the highest hopes of those who had wanted the cameras were met, but so were some of the worst fears of those who had not. It was pretty soon clear that there was less drug dealing in the areas covered by the CCTV. But those pockets out of sight of the cameras became havens of crime, mainly drug-dealing and prostitution. Two areas affected in this way were the Vicarage site, adjacent to All Saints' Church and Clydesdale Road. But events were to take an interesting turn towards the end of 1997, a few months after the cameras were installed.

The police say that it is much harder to put a stop to 'a closed drugs market', that is to say a market in which deals take place in private homes. So the first task of any anti-drugs policing campaign is to get the dealing on to the street and out of private homes. Drug dealers target weak members of the community, who are themselves often drug users, or may have been prostitutes but are not working anymore. By cajoling and ingratiating, they start to use their flats as places to deal and, if they are dealing in crack, as crack houses. A number of these opened in the area around All Saints Road. And many of them were in flats owned by the social landlords. The police could do little about activities in these crack houses unless they could find drugs when they 'busted' them. But the evidence could be quickly hidden. There was however one thing they could do. Police officers could be witnesses in civil actions to evict tenants by social landlords.

Eviction of a vulnerable tenant might seem harsh. In several instances the vulnerable tenant was persuaded to move out of their own volition giving the landlord, sometimes assisted by the police, the opportunity to evict the users of the flat, who were illegal occupiers once the tenants had moved, as well as being a nuisance to their neighbours.

Once these people had been evicted and the crack houses closed down, the drug dealing moved to the street. It had become an 'open market'. Having achieved that, the next task of the police was to get evidence of the dealing on video camera. In order to do that they had to get local people to accept police video cameras in their homes, something they were reluctant to do for fear of reprisals. In the view of the police this was an unjustified fear, but no less real for that. In addition to finding places to install cameras, the police had also to find a way of ensuring that the deals actually took place within sight of the cameras.

CCTV cameras moved the dealing to Clydesdale Road, very much to the irritation of the residents of that road whose perception was that the problem was getting worse, but in fact the geographical zone of operation was being narrowed down.

The residents of Clydesdale Road, fed up with constant drug dealing on their doorsteps launched an awareness campaign against drug abuse, 'Clydesdale Watch'. They were supported and advised by the Colville Project. Their campaign worked closely with the police informing them of the problems they were experiencing. Some residents were persuaded to have video cameras placed in their homes. And the evidence of dealing was slowly amassed.

One night at the end of 1997 the police swooped, arresting eight dealers. Unusually they had collected good quality evidence of dealing on video and not just possession of small qualities of drugs. All the arrested pleaded guilty and all were imprisoned.

All that remained to be done was to prevent the vacuum created being quickly filled by other dealers, because to begin with at least the buyers were still coming to the area, not knowing where the supply had gone. A few weeks of high profile policing – many officers on the street late at night in lime green fluorescent jackets – was enough to convince the buyers to take their trade elsewhere. Signs went up announcing that the area would continue to be under surveillance for drug use. Those signs stayed up for six months.

A joint sting

At first glance, this seems like a brilliant sting, but the police are the first to say that it could not have been achieved without the support of local people being willing to have cameras placed in their homes and alerting police to illegal activities on which they needed to collect evidence. The Colville Area Council was also crucial. The police could get a formal endorsement from the community for what they were doing. It was also there that they could test the strength of public feeling against the criminals and in support of the police.

Relations between the police and the local community in the Notting Hill area have not always been good in the past. Either traditional police methods were seen as heavy-handed or, stung by criticism, the police adopted a complete standoff, which felt to local residents like total neglect. There was a chance of another confrontation between police and community if they had adopted some of the tactics seen not only in Notting Hill in the late 1970s, but also in Brixton and Toxteth in the early 1980s. They had to win the community's support for swift, targeted action. The Colville Project and the Area Council and the All Saints Road Business Association gave them the means by which to do that.

Chapter five
Mutual communities

The word community, while always referring to what people have in common, is used in many different contexts. The most ordinary way, and the one applicable in the case of Colville, is when community refers to place. It then refers to the people who live in a place and, more than that, to people who have some bonds between them by reason of living there.

It is fashionable to say that neighbourhoods are no longer communities. Neighbours are strangers to each other. Family and friends are dispersed over great distances, sometimes across the globe. Socialising is done away from home, in city centres, or in pubs and bars near workplaces. Contact is maintained by telephone, not visiting. And when visits take place, they are curtailed by fast car journeys.

People's networks are now undoubtedly spread over greater geographical distances than has been the case in the past. Proximity to family and friends is not what it was. But that is a far cry from proclaiming the sad death of neighbourliness or to pronounce that communities have expired through neglect. If I am to argue that physical regeneration must be matched by social and community regeneration, a short exposition of the contemporary dynamics of community is required.

Stability of residence

If you go and live in a new place for a short time, as a transient you will be unusual if you develop any great attachment to the place or the people living there. More and more single, young professionals are moving into North Kensington. Some of them are the aforementioned 'trustafarians'. They are likely to be transients. But if they or you stay anywhere over a period of years you will be unusual if you do not feel to some extent that you belong there. The place becomes part of your identity. Stability of residence makes for identity within a community. People who stay in

Notting Hill or Knotty Ash end up by feeling they belong to Notting Hill or Knotty Ash and have a bond with others who do the same.

Stable residence is the first key. A powerful second element is added if the residence becomes multi-generational. Children are the seedbed of community. Though so tiny, babies embody a sense of hope for the future of the community. Mothers and fathers have something in common just because they have children. When the children are a little older they are often more sociable than their parents. If they have the chance to meet other children, at nursery or school, or if they play with each other in the square or in the park, they easily form friendships. They can then bring their parents together, often one of the strongest ties in a community.

Everywhere, the nursery or the primary school can be more than a school. It is a meeting place where people greet old friends and make new ones and because the children have become friends, there is something of an obligation on even the most shy parents to become tolerably social to one another. As most of the children at a primary school live fairly close, once they become friends, the parents do not have to go so far to see one another or to pick up and deliver children. Older children can be more relied on to make their own way to school. So the need for parental supervision no longer exists and the daily contact between parents ends. But by the time the children reach secondary school age, the parents may have become friends in their own right. Hence Abercrombie's assistance in the 1943 plan for London that urban villages should see primary schools as their epicentres. Hence also my suggestion in Chapter two that schools should form a key part of local multi-agency working.

In the Colville area the Colville nursery and primary school, at the geographical heart of the community in Lonsdale Road, has 265 pupils. Also nearby, St Mary of the Angels and St Stephen's are the two other primary schools attended by children living in Colville. They have 304 and 189 pupils respectively. They have all certainly been the wellspring of lasting social networks. I met people who came to the neighbourhood 30 years ago as tenants of private landlords, living then in grossly overcrowded conditions. They became tenants of Notting Hill or one of the other trusts in the late 1960s or early 1970s as I described in Chapter three. Since then their children have been through nursery, primary and secondary school in the neighbourhood. Their children are now adults, some married and moved away, but others still living in the neighbourhood, many still with their parents. One of the tenants indeed works in Colville nursery and has for many years, during which time her own child also attended the nursery. One of the children of another longstanding tenant is now an adult. She works at one of the local primary schools. All the people I spoke to whose children had attended primary schools in the area told us that delivering and collecting the children everyday had been an important way to get to know other people nearby.

But the children of long-established tenants are highly unlikely to be able to continue to live in the neighbourhood. Purchasing a place to live in North Kensington is the preserve only of the already wealthy and the young professional with a high and rising disposable income. Few children of social housing tenants fall into either of those categories. Nor are these longstanding residents likely to get social housing. In order to get social housing they would have to join the Council's register and if they were not in 'priority need', meaning that they are vulnerable, have a young family, are homeless or threatened with it, living in overcrowded conditions or without basic amenities, they are not likely to receive priority for social housing. And even if they did, there would be no guarantee that it would be in the Colville neighbourhood.

The allocation of social housing

Allocating social housing according to need is a beguilingly moral notion. In fact, constraints on the definition of need built up over the years mean that many people who are in need do not get housed, for example asylum seekers and people with mental health problems, whilst others who are part of the community, its history and stability and its future are displaced. Rationing social housing in this way seems ethical but is in fact destructive to the moral economy of help, support, friendship and family ties in the neighbourhood. This approach is predicated firstly on an apparently limitless number of people who need social housing and secondly an absolute constraint on the number who can have it. There are more and more places in the country where the notion of social housing shortage and the consequent need to ration is increasingly unconvincing. There is, as has been argued elsewhere by many people including myself, a need to place the building of successful multi-generational neighbourhoods at the heart not the periphery of social housing allocations. Otherwise the morality of meeting needs will be undermined by the immorality of throwing strangers together, sometimes in ways almost guaranteed to produce hostility.

In defining priority need, little attention has been paid to length of residence in a neighbourhood, ties of kinship or friendship, the spread of ages or generations, or the need for or the ability to give support to someone else in the community. Little wonder then that people who know not much about one another and feel no particular bond towards others nearby should also sometimes be the people who are casually destructive of other people's cars or homes, and indifferent to the impact that their noisy or anti-social behaviour has on fellow residents.

In the past there were 'Sons and Daughters' policies in the allocation of social housing. They were discredited by the suspicion of racism, and rightly so. But in the context of the very many races in North Kensington, it is highly unlikely that any system that gave some priority to local people in accessing local housing would disadvantage any ethnic group. Nor, if managed fairly and openly, need a system of local priorities undermine the commitment to meeting housing need. Meeting needs and sustaining neighbourhoods are not mutually exclusive, but they have become so in allocating social housing. We are all paying a high price; not just those denied a nearby home. Families and communities are scattered on a gale scale and the deleterious impact on social cohesion is profound and lasting. The Colville community lost one of its most active, able and neighbourly members who moved away when her housing association could not offer her a larger property in the area. Apparently approaching the other social landlords in the area who might have been able to help was not considered.

Some tenants moved away from the neighbourhood when their homes were nominated for reimprovement. So, even though smaller flats were enlarged by reducing the number of flats in the house as a whole, there was a net gain in housing available. This was filled in the traditional way through the local authority. It is a cause of some concern to most of the tenants who attended our focus groups. They are not suggesting that homeless people or people off the register should not be offered any housing in the neighbourhood. On the contrary they are concerned that people in need should not be unfairly excluded. But they are concerned that their family members, many of whom work in the Colville neighbourhood, have no alternative but to live in a distant part of London. It must surely be possible to strike a balance between competing and legitimate demands.

So here is another lesson for the future:

- A mechanism needs to be found by the Local Authority for continuing to meet need in social housing allocations, as well as to give priority to existing local residents which is fair and equitable. Many suggestions have been made in numerous reports. What all the suggestions have in common is the need to allocate social housing at the most local level possible, far more local than the entirety of a London borough.

Mutual aid

Once communities are established, providing they are not subverted by insensitive institutional interventions such as those above, their defining characteristic becomes 'mutual aid' – the belief and practice that more can be done together than can be done alone. The first and most humble meaning of mutual aid is more or less *simultaneous reciprocity*. A looks after B when B is ill and B looks after A when A is ill. The second and less humble meaning is *lagged reciprocity* (or 'cosmic book-keeping' as someone called it) when there are time lags in the process. The most fundamental time lag is when a parent looks after a child. It is at the time mostly one way aid, but later on there can be some return traffic of care and feeling when the child looks after the parent. This is mutual aid given and received at different points in the life cycle. Mutual aid in the prime of life is a repayment of the debts incurred in childhood and a downpayment on the care that might be needed in old age. Friends and neighbours might help one another too with no immediate return, but with a strong implicit presumption of help at an unspecified moment of future need.

The third and still less humble meaning is where mutuality becomes *multilateral*. A helps B. B helps C. C helps A. And so on. People can come together in pursuit of a shared interest, in which they will all have a stake, either now or in the future. And it is multilateral mutual aid that has been much in evidence in Colville.

Since 1992 community action and mutual aid have grown greatly. I have already given some examples of a greater, more shared sense of responsibility for the quality of life in the neighbourhood. This might be to do with one to one relationships between friends and neighbours; some started long ago through the nursery and the school. Others more recent, perhaps at My Beautiful Launderette, an important community meeting place. Or it might be to do with local voluntary responsibility for aspects of the physical environment such as the Adopt a Tree scheme and the Blooming Balconies competition or the Keep Colville Tidy clean-up days which were described in the last chapter. One resident made a comment about Colville Square, which would be equally applicable to the rest of the area, "Because it's nice, you feel like you want to keep it nice."

People came together to discuss the reimprovement programmes, usually at 108. So that was a chance to get to know people they may have been living near or by for many years but often with little contact. I was told of numerous small examples of mutuality and neighbourliness, visiting sick and housebound people that grew from these encounters.

One resident told us "the biggest gain from City Challenge was to bring people closer together." Another resident told us, "if you have a common purpose, it's quite close to having a common destiny". A third resident said, "if you are together, you have more power". Then there was organised voluntary activity such as the supplementary school, Pimento.

Pimento

The school was started by Family Services Unit in response to a strong feeling amongst local black parents that their children were being short-changed in the education system and therefore achieving a good deal less than their potential. The school is open from 4.30 to 6.30 for children between the ages of five and 13. About 60 children use the school and there is a long waiting list. Children receive education in maths, english and black perspectives. The school also runs summer play schemes.

Determined, organised voluntary effort is always impressive, more impressive even than people who do an excellent job for which they are paid. There is a point at which shared self-interest becomes altruism. It is the logical endpoint and counterweight to mutual aid. The school is run wholly by volunteers as are most of the very many supplementary schools in London and elsewhere. There are 20 in Kensington and Chelsea alone. Pimento has received some financial support only for rent from City Challenge, although funding for the future is uncertain.

Junior League of London

The Junior League of London is an example of altruism that I have referred to several times to which I must now give undivided attention. It is a branch of an international organisation of women committed to improving the community through voluntary service and developing the leadership capacity of women. They offer support to enhance the lives and capabilities of residents and to enable them to take an active role in their neighbourhood and its future. The League was invited to become a partner in the Colville Project following its work among families in temporary accommodation in Bayswater. The League has made an enormous contribution to the local community including organising the clean-up days, training people in growing window boxes for the Blooming Balconies Competition, setting up a Lenders Toy Library at Colville Nursery and providing an adventure climbing frame for Powis Square. They also organised leadership training events for local people.

The moral of all this is that even if a community has stability of residence, three generations and strong ties of mutuality and community action, there will always be a need for altruism, philanthropy and selflessness. No regeneration effort can thrive on money alone. Nor can it be sustained solely by self-help and mutual aid. Altruism, as well as government support, always has a part to play.

Police and community

One aspect of building strong communities is to strengthen relationships between local people and statutory and voluntary agencies. Everyone needs a shared sense of purpose. One of the most important relationships in an area where crime has been such a disfigurement to quality of life is between local people and the police. This had a chequered history in Notting Hill. The project was a good opportunity to carry on with the work of turning this around. The police became involved in the Colville Area Council, a multi-agency forum, and regularly attended the meetings throughout the life of the project. This created a space to keep residents informed about crime rates and the activities they were undertaking to combat crime. The Colville Area Council meetings were also opportunities for local residents to tell the police their concerns about crime in the neighbourhood.

Neighbourhood safety

The neighbourhood safety day was an event focused on what local residents could do for themselves and for each other to prevent crime. The Colville Area Council housing sub-group suggested a day of activities to promote community safety. Information was provided, demonstrations of self defence, road safety, interactive computer road safety tests, half-a-house safety methods and the stolen goods database.

The day was useful in itself for those who attended but the timing of the neighbourhood safety day was most fortuitous. It coincided with the installation of CCTV cameras throughout the area, which I have already described in Chapter four. The one on Westbourne Park Road at the bottom of All Saints Road had the impact of displacing drug dealers to Clydesdale Road, the very place where the neighbourhood safety day was being held. Because local residents were so conscious of these new problems, they turned out in force to the event. Through that, people who had not been involved before got to know of the work of the Colville Project and joined in with activities at 108. Notting Hill Housing Trust, whose tenants included many of those newly involved people, could then initiate a security action plan. The co-operation of some of the residents of Clydesdale Road also greatly assisted in collecting the evidence to arrest and convict the eight drug dealers in 1997 which I described in the last chapter.

The Vicarage site

The Vicarage site is two blocks of flats built in the 1970s on the site of the old Vicarage of All Saint's Church. There is also an open grassed area. Some prostitution and drug dealing had always been evident here, but once it became known that the eyes of the cameras could not see here, the problems became significantly worse. Residents complained of 'running the gauntlet' to get back to their homes. Lack of lighting, poor fencing, insecure main doors and door release systems that did not work, or worked too often, all exacerbated their fears. So a project team came together to look for solutions and funding for works. This led to security improvements to doors and better lighting, along with internal improvements.

Community action on drugs

Not all problems of crime and anti-social behaviour can be designed out. A community response is also needed. Before a community response can develop, strong relationships of trust and mutual purpose need to be struck, so it was thought that an early community response to a problem so treacherous and intractable as drug use in the neighbourhood would be difficult to generate and then sustain. Confidence was needed in the minds of local residents that they could take effective action.

Several years after the start of the Colville Project, in April 1997 the Community Resistance Against Substance Harm (CRASH) project was initiated as a partnership between Notting Hill Housing Trust, the Council, the All Saints Road Business and Community Association, local residents' associations, the Tenant Management Organisation, health authorities and other agencies working in the borough. It is a three-year programme funded through the Single Regeneration Budget, which aims to mobilise community groups to develop effective action to reduce the levels of nuisance, drug misuse and crime in their local neighbourhood.

CRASH's primary activities are to:

- Effectively advise and inform local communities.

- Encourage and support existing groups.

- Encourage and support the formation of new community organisations.

- Use information to inform community action.

The Colville Project's Tenant Participation Development Worker is running the community development aspect of the programme. The CRASH projects are being run in three other areas of Kensington and Chelsea. It is early days for CRASH, but hopes are high for such an important project.

Ledbury Road Traffic Campaign

In the chapter on improving the physical environment in the neighbourhood I described the campaign to calm traffic in the Canyon. There have also been other campaigns about traffic.

In early 1997 a local resident came into the Residents Information Centre at 108 Talbot Road to discuss her housing problems. Whilst there she also mentioned her concerns about Ledbury Road. From this discussion grew the Ledbury Road Traffic Campaign. The campaign aimed to make people more aware of the dangers of Ledbury Road and to push for improvements to the road to slow down traffic. They worked closely with the police and St Mary of the Angels School, who also presented a petition to the Council. Improvements now planned for the street and the police are working with the school on road safety issues.

Local involvement in licencing

Local people turned a disused garage into a car wash. Employed there were many previously unemployed young black men. This was a popular trouble-free service in the minds of local residents. In the mind, however, of an over-zealous planning officer it was an unpermitted activity requiring change-of-use authorisation. Local people came together at 108 and prevented the planning authorities from closing the car wash down.

At the same time, people from outside the neighbourhood took over a rundown pub and developed it into a restaurant and bar - Kassoulet. Local residents supported the Council's opposition to the late night music and dance licence that was sought. Not only was there local opposition, but a sustained campaign. Councillors turned down the application and the restaurant appealed to the Magistrates Court who decided to overturn the Council's decision. To fight this reversal, a partnership between local residents and the London Borough of Kensington and Chelsea was established. The Council's legal department took the appeal decision to the Crown

Court and 15 residents attended the hearing to speak on behalf of the community. The appeal was overturned and a hugely significant victory for local residents was won.

Two doors down a group of local people came together to open a café - Coins. They have received the support and patronage of local people. When they opened they did not have an evening licence and swore that they would not seek one. Now that the daytime business has gone so well, they are talking about seeking an evening licence and there is no local opposition. They endeared themselves further to the community by giving the café over to be used by the Black and Minority Ethnic Residents' Group (BMER) to hold two reminiscence evenings. The perception that they are of the community and support local people has evidently all owed them a more flexible licence to operate.

It would seem from these three examples that local residents, round the epicentre of the Residents Information Centre at 108, have taken on an informal licensing role, and one of their key criteria is whether or not the proprietors of new business are local people. So there is an informal mutual obligation here - to encourage economic activity by local people and in return not to cause a nuisance to local residents.

A structure for community involvement

In all sectors, public, private and voluntary, there is a growing emphasis on the need to recognise the perspectives of all stakeholders in planning and decision-making and on building the different perspectives into the structure. There is also a growing recognition of the need for multi-agency working, indeed that was an underlying principle behind City Challenge.

A feature of the Colville neighbourhood that I have already referred to is the range of landlords and tenure arrangements. A further complexity was the diversity of issues on which the views of local people and organisations were to be sought – reimprovement to homes, the environment, crime, drugs, security, traffic, rubbish, town planning and licencing, open spaces. So one structure was needed to reflect the range of interests and subjects. The solution was inventive and fair.

The tenants of each of the social housing landlords formed themselves into a residents association – one each for Notting Hill Housing Association tenants, Kensington Housing Trust tenants, and one each for tenants of the TMO, private residents and the Black and Minority Ethnic Residents.

Figure 6: A structure for tenant and resident involvement in Colville

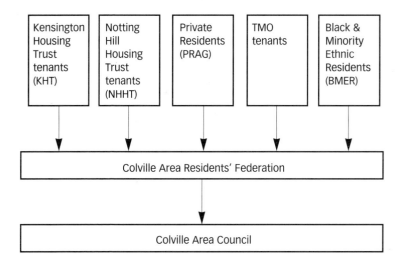

I have hopefully shown that in all its manifestations - within the family, amongst neighbours, between local people and local organisations, in the formation of self-help groups and in building democratic local structures – the community is alive and well in Colville. Indeed the work of 108 and the Colville Project greatly strengthened the ties between the people in the area and that, with a lubricating injection of altruism, has encouraged all of the activities described. Now that City Challenge funding is at an end, can these ties be sustained? Time will tell, but I have some practical suggestions as to how this might achieved to make in Chapter eight.

Chapter six
Arrival, struggle, inclusion - The question of race

In *The Politics* Aristotle notes, "A city is composed of different kinds of men; similar men cannot bring a city into existence." Perhaps he would have included women if he were writing now. After America, Britain is the most racially diverse nation in the world and London is the most racially diverse city in Britain. There are 37 communities in London with more than 10,000 people, including people from Canada, Portugal, Spain, Ghana, Italy, Poland, Turkey, Iran, Mauritius, Philippines, Japan and New Zealand. Of less than 10,000 people there are many more communities. Nearly half of Britain's ethnic minority population lives in London. One in five of London's population is from an ethnic group.

North Kensington is one of the most racially diverse neighbourhoods in London with an ethnic minority population of 26,000 speaking a total of 90 different languages. After English, Arabic is the most commonly spoken language in the North Kensington area.

Table 1: Ethnicity in Colville

Ethnic group	Size of population in Colville per cent
White	75
Black Caribbean	8.6
Black African	4
Black Other	2.5
Indian	1.3
Pakistani	0.4
Bangladeshi	0.4
Chinese	0.7
Asian other	2.7
Other (mainly from North Africa and the Maghreb)	4.6

Source: 1991 Census

81

Arrival and losing the gift of dreams

Behind these baldly stated facts is a complex history. Racial diversity has not been an untarnished blessing, for white or for black people. Many black people came to London thinking it was a place that they knew very well from their colonial education back home. But as the great writer V.S Naipaul described in his wonderful book describing his own arrival in West London, *The Enigma of Arrival*, they found a city that was strange and unknown – in its style of houses, even in the names of its districts, and most of all in the decidedly mixed attitudes of its people. The discomfort experienced when faced with this strangeness, sometimes veering into hostility, was very great. Many, saddened by these experiences, lost the gift of fantasy, the dream of the future, the sense of a far-off place where they thought they were going. For some no further dream was possible. These personal disappointments and depredations, made much worse by the intolerance of some of those amongst whom they arrived, were by and by to produce a conflagration.

Scars on the soul

On 17 August 1958 a white crowd smashed the windows of a house occupied by black people in Stowe Road, Shepherd's Bush. A few days later a black man was savagely attacked in a pub in North Kensington by white men who battered him with metal dustbin lids and jabbed him with broken milk bottles. Over a wide area, gangs of white teenagers armed with iron bars, sticks and knives went, as they put it, 'nigger-hunting'. By the end of August brawls, disturbances and racial attacks were a daily and nightly feature of life in North Kensington. The climax came at the beginning of September. After an open air fascist meeting a crowd of hundreds of white youths surged through the area 'in an excited state'. They ran through the streets shouting "let's get the niggers", knocking down all in their way, smashing windows as they went. In May 1959 a West Indian carpenter, Kelso Cochrane, was stabbed to death in a North Kensington street. His murderer was never found. These events left a scar on the soul of the community.

Struggle

Black political organisation began then in North Kensington and has not ceased since despite some heavy-handed attempts at suppression in the 1970s. When a demonstration took place in August 1970 against repeated police raids on the Mangrove restaurant in All Saints Road, a meeting-place of black radicals, the police unhesitatingly picked out the organisers and arrested them. Through a skilful defence, so skilful in fact that the provisions that the defence was based on have been 'modernised' out of legal existence, the Mangrove Nine were acquitted.

Carnival should be a celebration of urban cultural diversity as it is in many cities across the world but the Notting Hill Carnival became the scene of contestation. Things reached a head at the Carnival of 1976. A full-blown confrontation flashed between the police and people they suspected of crimes. Many years were to pass before good relations were once more established between black people and the police. And the community's soul had a further scar.

Diversity

But other strands of racial diversity have not proved so negative. Quite, in fact, the contrary. Marginality from the cultural mainstream has become a highly creative space in many industries, notably the music industry, which has deep roots in the Notting Hill area. On his arrival in Britain Daddy Peckings set up Pecking's Studio One record shop in West London. He was the first person to sell reggae and its antecedents – bluebeat, ska and rocksteady – in Britain. The fledgling sound system culture of urban Jamaica was transplanted into Britain during the 1950s and on his arrival Peckings began to supply records to Duke Vin of Ladbroke Grove, the first sound system in this country.

Many of the early debates about race relations assumed that assimilation and integration were the keys to racial harmony. When black children became black adults they would be, in cultural terms, like white young adults in all things but colour. Uniformity was seen as the route to equality. In fact, many black and minority ethnic people have retained many of the cultural traditions drawn from, though altered by time, their place of origin – language, religion, music, family loyalty and so on into the second and third generations. It has now come to be accepted that not only should diversity be tolerated, but celebrated.

In the 1980s and 1990s things multi-cultural have taken a new twist. Very far from young black people becoming like young white people, the converse has happened. Youth culture in the cities is in large measure defined by black cultural expressions, at least until Britpop came along. Meanwhile young black people have found opportunities not only to move between what might be called their culture of origin and white British culture, but also between ethnic cultures. So, now we have Asian rap artists for example. Double consciousness has arrived. Ethnic identities are not pure or static, or conservative, or 'expat'. In fact they change in new circumstances or by sharing social space with other heritages and influences. Moreover this also challenges existing conceptions of Britishness. Here is the critic Stuart Hall,

> "Within culture, marginality, though it remains peripheral to the broader mainstream, has never been such a productive space as it is now. And that is not simply the opening within the dominance of space that those outside it can occupy. It is also the result of the cultural politics of difference, of the struggles around difference, of the production of new identities, of the appearance of new subjects on the political and cultural stage."

But this too has had its downside. Young, black men have been stereotyped as violent and disruptive, challenging the authority of teachers and the police; or they have been praised and emulated as macho, 'cool' and exemplars of youth culture. The success of young black men as leaders of youth culture and fashion could be seen as socially self-defeating for it has taken them away from a 'classroom culture' to a 'street culture'. And some of the worst of that street culture made its unmistakable presence known in drug dealing and the rise of crack houses in the Colville neighbourhood that I have already described.

Inclusion

The murder of Kelso Cochrane in 1958 was the first 'race moment' in North Kensington. Twenty years and one generation later, the disorder at the Notting Hill Carnival in 1976 was the second 'race moment'. It is very probable that June 1998, a further 20 years on, will come to be seen as the third moment. But it is one of a wholly different nature to the previous two, one of tradition and diversity celebrated in the context of a new inclusion. The symbolic event is the Multi-Cultural History Week held in June 1998. And the method by which this has come about is the Black and Minority Ethnic Residents' Group (BMER) that was initiated by the Colville Project. Before I describe the Multi-Cultural History Week and its importance a little background is needed.

BMER

In 1993 the staff recognised that few of the local black residents attended the consultation meetings about improving homes and the environment. Even those black people who did attend contributed little. So Notting Hill's Tenant Participation Worker initiated BMER. The object was not to run parallel structures for consultation with black people, but to encourage and empower people to participate in the other structures, as well as to discuss the specific concerns of local black and minority ethnic residents.

The group has grown and grown and the meetings are now held frequently. They are lively, sometimes a little too lively and sometimes a little too long. They involve all sorts of black people from the neighbourhood. That is one of the distinguishing marks of BMER. Some of the people who attend are professionals, articulate and confident. Others are long time community activists who have been involved in the struggle for many a summer and some dark winters. But there are also new arrivals, some of whom speak no English, but nonetheless value the social contact and the sense of friendly support.

The make-up of the group is a crucial development. It is diversity within diversity. The agenda of the group is sometimes political, but it is not only politicos who become involved. Its agenda is also social, but nonetheless activists attend. And the group is not only outwardly focused on influencing the Council and other local organisations. It is also a source of mutual support to its members. In its range of activities and its inclusivity it is an unremarked landmark of black organisation. And its potential prototypical power should not be lost.

Some other distinctive characteristics mark the group out. Firstly it has received much encouragement and support from senior white staff in a largely white organisation, Notting Hill Housing Trust. Secondly, the Tenant Participation Worker, and some of the members, have the gift of being able to talk to anyone – the Chief of Police, drug dealers, gunmen, councillors, business people. This is an impressive and essential quality. The terms of engagement have changed. For example, members of BMER have met with Scotland Yard, who not so long ago would have been seen as the enemy, or in popular vernacular, 'Babylon'.

The most powerful impact of BMER has been to give black residents greater confidence, derived from one another, to work at all levels of the system to improve their own and other people's lots. No longer are they the grateful and passive recipients of services that they have no power to influence. As one black resident told us, the situation previously was, "Our presence was as good as it gets. You've got a flat. You should be happy." Now local black residents come together with one another and comments are overheard such as, "Did you see this in the paper. We can send off for this." People feel more confident to challenge, not just local services such as housing benefit and social services, but on a wider national canvas too – on matters such as asylum and immigration law, the policies of the Housing Corporation, discrimination in the Criminal Justice System, and many others besides.

There are some important lessons here:

- It may sometimes be necessary to have separate structures as a way of involving black people in mainstream decision making.

- Those structures need to be inclusive and social, as well as formal and business-like.

- Black people come together not simply to influence or work with mainstream associations. Black groups are also an important source of mutual aid and mentoring through generations and across social class.

- Leadership and support is required from white people in mainstream organisations.

- Workers with confidence and exceptional interpersonal skills are needed who can bring people together, from all parts of society, without fear or favour. These gifts are more critical than the more prosaic qualities required for mainstream housing management, though they would not go amiss there either.

Multi-Cultural History Week

As I have said it is twenty years since the last race moment in Notting Hill, the disorder at the 1976 carnival. A different generation brought together Multi-Cultural History Week in June 1998. The first two reminiscence evenings held at Coins café in Talbot Road brought together 80 people at each meeting. An air of reflection and nostalgia prevailed as the group reclaimed a hidden past behind the barricades of anger and struggle. A more gentle history came out of bewilderment on arrival, ameliorated in some measure by the friendship and love of friends and relatives from home already here. And over the subsequent years, the growth of a musical and performance culture, which reaches its apotheosis once a year at Carnival. A new generation is more ambitious, with double consciousness, wanting to be marginal and central. Not happy with shouting from the margins of the struggle. But equally reluctant to lose the sense of that part of the past, its ironies and paradoxes celebrated not least in a new generation of black comedians, writers and musicians.

A more complex, integrated, multi-layered and multi-faceted sense of the past is wanted, so that the true complexity of the past can feed, inform and reassure positively the uncertainties and complexities of what is yet to come.

The Mutli-Cultural History Week attracted big crowds of local people, white as well as black. The Tabernacle, where most of the events were held, was packed with two to three hundred people every night. Events included:

- Role Models Gallery – successful celebrities and role models from ethnic communities talk about their lives;

- 'Fashion through the Ages' show;

- An open evening entitled 'How did we get here and where are we going?' looking at the different aspects of Black culture in England over the past 50 years;

- African dancing and steel band performances;

- Poetry evening and comedy night;

- Youth activities – such as a performance arts and modern dance workshops;

- A debate about the future of multi-cultural education.

'We people who are darker than blue'

One can see from the foregoing list of activities a sense of a complex history being reclaimed, not just one of struggle and strife, but of fashion, music, poetry, storytelling, humour and dance. Anyone attending the events would have been struck by the presence of a new generation of young black people, in their teens and twenties, who see themselves differently in many ways to their older friends and relations. They have begun, 50 years after the arrival of the *Windrush*, to grasp tentatively the complex and confusing meaning of being Black and British. They challenge more directly the ambiguities of the notion of 'home' in an increasingly diasporic world.

But we must not forget, whilst recognising the changes that have occurred and are still taking place, the continuing presence of mindless racial hatred and the real possibility of passive collusion by the authorities. Forty years after the unsolved murder of Kelso Cochrane, a harmless Antiguan carpenter, the racist murder of Stephen Lawrence, an equally harmless school boy, looks likely to be unsolved too. Not everything has changed, and not all for the better.

Chapter seven
Two villages: The local economy

A village divided

"Two nations: between whom there is no intercourse and no sympathy; who are as ignorant of each other's habit, thoughts, and feelings, as if they were dwellers in different zones, or inhabitants of different planets; who are formed by a different breeding, are fed by a different food, are ordered by different manners, and are not governed by the same laws".

"You speak of" - said Egremont hesitatingly, "the rich and the poor?"

This was Disraeli's novel, *Sybil*, written in 1845, in which the notion of 'two nations' first surfaced. It has long since been taken into the political discourse. But since Disraeli's time it is not two nations that we have become, but two cities, two towns and two villages.

In the last 20 years the most poor have grown even poorer as the benefit system has been chipped away at, and incomes amongst the working population have risen. Falling unemployment in the early 1990s has reversed in small ways the trend to ever greater inequality. Even more marked than the growth of absolute poverty is the growth of absolute wealth. The problem is one of social polarisation and not just growing poverty. The two structural economic trends are not easy to separate. Among households with children the divergence of income has been more pronounced than for other households. For the poorest 20 per cent their disposal income after housing costs (which have risen much faster than any other aspect of the household budget) fell on average from £88 per week in 1979 to £78 per week in 1993.

At the other extreme, for the richest 20 per cent over the same period, weekly income rose from £232 to £359 per week. In less than a generation, our nation has converted inequality between rich and poor from a ratio of 4:1 to a ratio of 7:1.

And nowhere have these changes been more marked than in London. The presence of a large number of people with high incomes in the capital skews average figures upwards. Gross weekly average household income was £435.30 in London in 1994/5. This is about 20 per cent higher than the national figure of £375.60. Thirty-five per cent of London households had an income of more than £475 per week compared with 28 per cent in the rest of the country. At the other end of the scale 22 per cent of households in the capital had a gross income below £125 per week in 1994/1995 – a figure similar to the country as a whole.

Although still the wealthiest city in the country, London is home to some of the nation's most deprived people. Poverty in London has intensified. More than one in six people receive income support (1994). In 1989 this figure was one in ten. Including partners and children, over 1.5 million Londoners rely on income support. In the UK around one in four of the workforce experienced a spell of unemployment between April 1992 and October 1995. In London it was one in three – around 1.4 million people. In July 1996, 365,000 Londoners were unemployed. Forty-three per cent of them had been unemployed for more than a year.

The people of Colville experience greater deprivation than their near neighbours across Kensington and Chelsea. So, to take just one indicator, in July 1996, 20.5 per cent of men and 12.9 per cent of women in Colville were unemployed. In the borough as a whole, 11.8 per cent of men and 7 per cent of women were unemployed.

Virtually everywhere in London rich people live alongside poor people, so in that sense this is not a news item. But the thing about North Kensington is that we have here not just the rich and the poor, but the very poor – homeless people, alcoholics, drug addicts – beside the very rich. Some feel that this makes Colville two villages. The inhabitants of the rich village have little to do with the inhabitants to the poor.

This is, of course, not a phenomenon confined to London. As Charles Landry and Frances Bianchini put it in *The Creative City*,

> "The cities which are the centres of the new global knowledge economy – London, New York, Frankfurt, Tokyo and Los Angeles – are increasingly socially fragmented, their labour markets divided between highly paid managers, technologists and professionals skilled in transitional law, government and business procedures, and employees – many of whom are women or from ethnic minorities – in less skilled, low paid, low status and often part-time service jobs."

If we do not take care, this will continue to be the situation in North Kensington. Local people do not get work in new businesses, nor do they use the new bars and restaurants. Those are for people who come into the neighbourhood to visit and then leave again. The money they spend whilst they are there goes into the hands of the people who work in and own these new businesses, and, of course, they too do not live or, more crucially, spend money in the neighbourhood. So the money only changes hands once and then leaves the area, making no contribution to speak of to the local economy. In middle class areas money may pass through five or six pairs of hands before leaving the area. So one goal must be to get the money coming in to the area to stay in the area. It needs to be spent in ways that pass into the hands of local people. The implication of this is for local people to work in the new local businesses. In order for new businesses to employ local people a tolerant and trusting relationship is needed and this will need to be fostered.

Most people get jobs through contacts. Most jobs are not advertised and are filled by word of mouth, especially in smaller businesses and in catering and retail. Moreover most people get jobs not through working their strong contacts, their family, immediate neighbours and very old friends, but through people they know less well, such as former colleagues, acquaintances and friends of friends. It is not that these contacts lead people directly to offers of jobs, but to information, to opportunities, to favours and, in some situations, to patronage.

Colville had no natural large employers; rather it had small businesses and shops employing few people alongside the abundance of lone artisans, craftspeople, who thrived in the area. So the strategy for tackling the economic problems of the Colville area could not be a formal one. The informal approach was two fold using local labour and providing support and advice for businesses and individuals.

Local labour

Womens' Education in Building (WEB) undertook the refurbishment of the Residents' Information Centre at 108. Hammersmith and Fulham Building Training Course carried out the works I have described to Colville Alley. A local artist/craftsman was involved with a number of projects; constructing the community notice boards, designing the Colville Project logo and letterhead and signwriting at the Residents' Information Centre. In the improvements to the Canyon, the short-list of architects in the competition to undertake the design work was drawn up from local companies with experience in local community projects. All jobs at the Colville project were advertised locally and at least one local residents' representative was on each interview panel. The Colville Project Co-ordinator was a local resident.

Other schemes were explored such as using only local labour contractors in the major works schemes and employing local trainees as part of the major works contracts. These ran into problems because of the open-list policy of Notting Hill Housing Trust and the fact that the very nature of the Colville Project required smaller, tenant-friendly contracts. These companies found it impossible to accommodate new trainees specifically for Colville.

Local business

As part of the informal strategy for generating local employment the project sought to encourage and support local businesses. Residents interested in starting new businesses came to 108 for advice. The central location of

108 meant that businesses thinking of coming to the area often came there to sound out their ideas, for example, a local family long resident in the neighbourhood who were already active at the Colville Project, came to 108 to get advice about starting a business. The staff at 108 assisted them with planning issues and also helped them find suitable premises for a restaurant. The project supported their application to lease a property in All Saints Road and persuaded Notting Hill Housing Trust that they would be suitable tenants. The restaurant opened in December 1996.

Coins Coffee Shop

105-107 Talbot Road was a large, derelict shop that, over the years, had been the subject of a number of bids for improvement, all of which had fallen through. A local resident wanted to turn the premises into a coffee shop but was running into difficulties changing the planning use of the premises. The project and residents were consulted and supported the planning application provided that a late night licence was not applied for and the café was to shut early evening. The planning permission was awarded and the coffee shop has flourished. The owners are now applying for an evening licence with the support of residents, despite their initial reluctance as I described in Chapter five.

Marios

A local security firm wanted to be put on Notting Hill Housing Trust's list of contractors but were having difficulties meeting the strict requirements. The Colville Project helped them to make a successful application to the list.

JB's Carwash

Local people turned a disused garage into a car washing business which employed many young, black men who had previously been unemployed. Local residents were very supportive of the service and came together to successfully oppose its closure by the planning authority, again as mentioned in Chapter five.

Swapping power

A local resident, involved in the project, was advised and given valuable contacts for their business, a magazine and swapping service for council and housing association tenants. The scheme was launched in early 1998.

Setting up 108

Local businesses also made an invaluable contribution to setting up 108. When approached with the idea of sponsoring 108, staff were astounded at the positive way in which the local businesses wanted to support the project. Donations were made of shelving, noticeboards, the central-heating system, computers, and carpets, right down to the doormat. Those sponsoring 108 recognised the need for the Centre, and over the years many continued to support its activities, including for example the Multi-Cultural History week in June 1998.

Training and support of residents

The diversified economy of the area did not encourage a top-down local employment strategy. Most of the businesses, old and new, are too small-scale. The plan therefore was to empower individuals to allow them to 'plug into' the employment system. The staff looked at the potential and aspirations of individuals, and offered support and practical assistance. For example:

* A local young man was interested in working with young people. He was put in touch with the Project's contact at the youth department and is now qualifying to become a youth worker.

* A skilled local embroiderer who wanted to gain a teaching qualification but did not have the confidence to do it. She was advised how to gain funding and where to find courses but also encouraged about her own ability. She has now gained a teaching qualification.

- A local woman went on the Junior League Leadership and Communication course which, in her own words, "inspired and gave me confidence to apply for better jobs." She got the job she had been looking for.

- A local woman who played a prominent role in the beginning of the project said that her experiences led her to take on professional training.

For the future

This highly dispersed modern, urban economy of small businesses producing high value services for global customers creates many employment opportunities for local people, but they need to be harnessed. Otherwise the money that comes into the area can quickly leave as I have said. Retailers of high added value goods are moving near to the Colville area with increased rapidity. The fashion stores Paul Smith and Agnes B are recent arrivals nearby. Creative approaches to these firms could offer employment opportunities for local people. But they could also offer far more, like the support of local businesses for the setting up of 108.

Corporate citizenship and the need to grow smaller businesses are both growing concerns across Britain. The influential inquiry by the Royal Society of Arts, *Tomorrow's Company*, noted that there is a growing recognition by UK businesses that the community in general – as well as government in particular – has a major influence on its ability to compete successfully. The relationship with the local community is set, in the view of the inquiry, to play a more integral part in core business decisions as companies learn to recognise the importance of earning the approval of the community and government. In order to maintain their licence to operate and preserve their right to be heard, consistency between words and actions is needed which is inherent in an inclusive approach to all business relationships.

Nor are these new concerns only for the Royal Dutch Shells and the Marks and Spencers. The same inquiry also concluded that to reverse the relative decline of the UK economy, Britain needs to add to the growing number of excellent smaller businesses. We need more boldly managed, robustly financed, and internationally ambitious business start ups, which build on the proven British ability to innovate.

As with so many other things, the Colville neighbourhood finds itself once more at the cutting edge of social change. The future of the work that goes on in 108 must take in a wider agenda. The job is not just to encourage the use of local labour, the gains from which, while important, are always marginal. The bigger job is to ensure that the growing prosperity of some in the area finds its way back into the local community. As we have already seen, if local businesses need a formal licence, or a more informal licence to operate, they will need the support of local people. Kassoulet, having lost its informal licence to operate in the minds of local people, then found itself unable to get a formal licence to operate.

These contacts with local businesses will need careful nurturing. They may be slow to take root. But the payback for many not so well off local people may prove enormous. In the face of economic structural change, the possibility of a new social partnership comes into view. Diverse local people, working in diverse local businesses serving needs and adding value across the world. Establishing that social partnership between local businesses and local people is a major priority for the future work of the Colville Project and in the next chapter I suggest some ways to make this happen. And that partnership will be greatly facilitated by building the capacity of local people to be equal partners. To gain employment, people need to be employable with the right skills and crucially, the right attitudes. Building that capacity and employability is necessary not just for local prosperity but for social cohesion.

Chapter eight

Sustaining the impact: The Mutual Aid Compact

Much has been achieved at Colville since 1992. And much has been learnt. There are lessons to be applied in many places where similar approaches to social, physical and economic regeneration are needed. But there are still many things to be done here. Some of them are more of the same. Many homes still need improvement. There is still much to be done on energy efficiency, security, the physical environment, traffic management and so on. The impetus should not be lost. But there is a risk that it will be. City Challenge created two imperatives, which have now disappeared – time and money. Whatever was to be done had to be done in five years for that was how long the money would be available. So what is to be done in the absence of these imperatives? How can the positives be sustained in the community spirit, the renascent village atmosphere that was so often described to us? A great deal could be done and I want to propose a mechanism for doing it.

Chris Argyris, Emeritus Professor at Harvard University has drawn a useful and important distinction between different kinds of commitment. His work is based on seeking to transform organisations, but it can as readily be applied to the public and social realm.

He says that commitment is about generating human energy and activating the human mind. Human beings can commit themselves in two fundamentally different ways: externally and internally. *External commitment* is what an organisation or a society gets when workers have little control over their destinies. The less power people have to shape their lives, the less commitment they will have. When the Berlin Wall came down, a routine way of life came to an end for

East German workers. Over the years before that East Germans had learned how to do the minimum required of them. To do any more was risky. Theirs was solely an external commitment.

The other kind of commitment is *internal commitment*. If the leaders of organisations or societies want people to take more responsibility for their own destiny, they must encourage individuals and groups to be committed to a particular person, place or project for their own reasons and based on their personal values.

These differences could be summed up:

External Commitment	Internal Commitment
• Tasks defined and described by others	• Individuals define tasks
• Behaviour required defined by others	• Behaviour required appropriate to individual
• Goals set by leaders	• Goals set jointly and collaboratively
• Importance of goal defined by leaders	• Importance of goal defined by individuals

To these two kinds of commitment I would add a third - *mutual commitment* as shown in Figure 7:

Figure 7: Mutual commitment

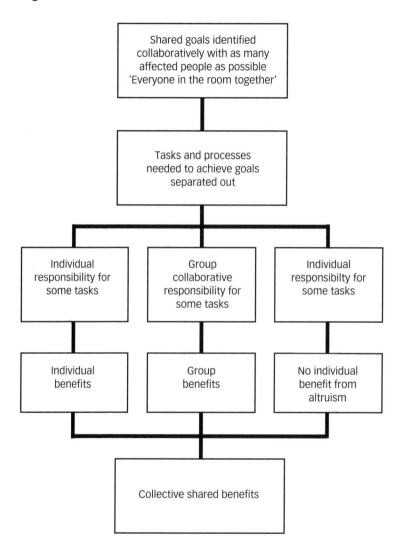

In order to facilitate the strengthening of this mutual commitment, I want to propose that local residents be asked to sign a *Mutual Aid Compact*. It could be signed by local residents and local businesses and take the form shown in Figure 8.

Figure 8: The Mutual Aid Compact

THE MUTUAL AID COMPACT

If the community of Colville is to be a community based on mutual respect it needs to be:

- A place where there is respect for other's property, where all crime affecting people and property is kept to a minimum;

- A place where there is respect for the environment, ensuring that it is clean and that public areas are kept in good order;

- A place where there is respect for other people's different lifestyles;

- A place where there is respect for open spaces which are safe and pleasant for children to play in and young people and others to meet;

- A place where people already know, or get to know and support one another, especially providing support to those in need of the greatest assistance, such as old or disabled people;

- A place where local people have local employment opportunities.

I am/my organisation is willing to make a contribution to the mutual aid needed to create and sustain this community.

I am/my organisation is willing to help my neighbour, or someone else living nearby, with practical support for things they cannot do easily for themselves, or by joining a group dedicated to encouraging self-help or to giving practical support, or by facilitating local employment.

I am willing to make the annual mutual aid commitment to this community, identifying what I or my organisation can offer to the community, and what support I need.

Signed

....

I am not proposing coercion. No one would have to sign. Nor would there be any suggestion of legal enforceability. Does this mean it would be pointless? Not at all. It would be a prompt for new expectations. The object is to build up a new body of practice amongst local residents that will have the persuasive force of *custom*. The chances of the Mutual Aid Compact creating a new custom would be less if we were seeking something entirely new. We are not. Informal mutual aid, in and out of families and neighbourhoods, is nothing new, as we have already seen in many examples in Colville. What I am seeking is to add to it. Persuasion should never be undervalued as a means of support for custom and as a means of bringing about a new custom.

But to persuade needs to be someone's responsibility if mutual aid is to grow. The staff at 108 could see all the people who had signed the Compact, perhaps once a year, and discuss with them what they might be prepared to do for other local residents or local services, such as Adopt a Tree, Keep Colville Tidy or becoming involved in the work of the Junior League. People could then be put in touch with a local organisation or group of local people whose interests or concerns they share. If none such exist, the staff could assist in setting up new ones, as they already have, for example, with BMER and Ledbury Road Traffic Campaign

For some public services, where external commitment has diminished and funds are likely to continue to be in short supply, such as maintaining the quality of public open spaces like Colville and Powis Squares, and it has not been replaced by internal commitment, there is a need for a new mutual commitment. Services provided at a poor standard - certainly not at one that reflects contemporary consumer expectations, could and should be transferred from the public, not to the private, but to the mutual. And the Mutual Aid Compact might be the means by which that transfer could be brought about.

If local businesses can be persuaded by the staff of the Colville Project to be more active participants in the life of the neighbourhood, they too could sign the Mutual Aid Compact. And they could fulfil their self-sought obligation by supporting local community activities, events and projects, as they have with the Multi-Cultural History Week and with 108. They could also offer training and employment opportunities to local people, retaining to the neighbourhood the benefits of local prosperity. And by and by the Mutual Aid Compact might facilitate the local licence to operate that I discussed in the last chapter.

The Mutual Aid Compact might contribute to reinforcing and creating neighbourly customs and, in that way, sustain the fragile spirit of community that has been engendered over the last five years. It would be a simple, practical means to bring an ideal nearer to being a reality, seeking to use a formal method to bring about more informal mutual aid. Such approaches are taking hold elsewhere in Britain, in Bradford and Stepney for example, so there is good reason to hope that they might do the same in Colville.

Chapter nine
Lessons learnt

Throughout this book I have argued that great social and economic changes can be seen in microcosm in the Colville neighbourhood, in the environment and in the many ways that people live their lives. What happens in the world happens here. Here for these purposes is Colville, but here could almost certainly be anywhere. And it is not only geography, but also history. The full impact of changes that started long ago are only now felt; and felt in consequences that were neither predicted, nor very often intended. So to refer to the example given in Chapter three, the purpose of central heating was to keep the whole house warm, not just one or two rooms as had hitherto always been the case. One of the consequences was that children withdrew into their private spaces. Was that a good or a bad thing? It meant they could do their homework in peace but it attenuated family life. So it was both good and bad.

All over the developed world the 1980s and 1990s saw a determined attempt to make changes which sought to respond to step changes in society, technology, politics and economics. A step change in government was looked for and the means were manifold - increasing competition between and within state sector and voluntary sector institutions, privatisation, increased responsibilities on employers and citizens. All the reforms were meant to get more services from less public spending. An international tax revolt was going on across the middle classes. Any political party that announced its intention to put up taxes was apparently doomed to defeat at the polls. So reducing expenditure on public services while seeking to match raising consumer expectations was an unavoidable political imperative.

These reforms arrested the growth of government, but failed to reverse it, introduced new efficiencies, made public sector managers more effective and accountable, and encouraged some, though by no means enough, innovation in the services delivered and the manner of the delivery.

But, as we have seen in Colville, all of the reforms failed to address some of people's most urgent concerns. The old questions of overcrowding, rapacious landlordism and poor or non-existent amenities had by the early 1990s been largely answered. But new questions were posed. How were we to address the intractable 'wicked' issues - rising crime, unemployment, a degraded environment and decayed publicly owned buildings? The Colville Project sought to address these concerns holistically and given below are the lessons learnt from these experiences.

A democratic neighbourhood base

The need for a neighbourhood base for regeneration is paramount. This base should work with all local people, not just the tenants of one or other landlord, or the users of one or other services. The staff should be constant, work holistically with all people's needs, work as a team, sharing information, so that local people are happy to talk to any of them, and they should seek out themes and patterns around which to build local collective responses, campaigns and organisations.

The neighbourhood centre should also be a focus for local democratic accountability. Operating in a smaller community then a local authority area, structures are needed to involve all local individuals, groups and organisations in a transparent and accountable way. The church and primary schools are key stakeholders who are all too often not involved. The use of public money needs democratic and accountable structures. Local people need to know what is going on. But they also need to know who is taking the decisions. Openness matters alongside leadership and effectiveness.

Investing in capacity building is an essential ingredient in an effective plan for regeneration. This might include funding and resources for training, development workers or consultancy support, premises and equipment, assistance with organisational development, developing networks and structures to support community organisations.

Funding is not always available at the beginning of a new campaign or initiative. The need for action is identified. The extent of need is then identified and then funds are found. The process is not opportunistic, but responsive.

In mainstream housing management, in and out of the urban regeneration context, tenants want a holistic, person-centered service. They want continuity and familiarity of staff teams. They also want friendly, comfortable offices and minimal use of appointments and voice mails. Informality and efficiency are not necessarily mutually exclusive.

Improving homes

Don't underestimate the difficulties of working around tenants in carrying out reimprovement works, especially in scattered converted property. Be imaginative about decanting solutions during reimprovement works. Otherwise you are in for a long hard search.

Clearly define and state the parameters of tenant choice and involvement in the reimprovement of their home. Have a named individual to manage the relationship between the tenant and everyone else involved in the reimprovement. Without a one-stop contact, muddle and disappointment will surely ensue - liaison through one named person is needed throughout the contract, not just while it is being planned. Establish a forum for setting consistent standards and dealing with difficulties.

Environmental improvements

When it comes to environmental improvements, unlike when improving tenants' homes, start with a blank sheet of paper. Define responsibilities, commitments and boundaries between local agencies clearly at an early stage. Be realistic about the length of time that will be needed to achieve a consensus or, at least a compromise between the various interests in the local community. Be realistic also about the length of time the works are going to take and establish the level of local consultation – will residents decide or advise?

Don't offer to consult people unless you intend to listen to their views. If there are limits to what can be afforded or achieved, set out those limits at the beginning of the process.

Focus on the needs of children and old people in planning environmental improvements. If they are satisfied, adults, particularly working adults, are also likely to be satisfied. Use a community architect/landscape architect and other advisors, who are used to working with community groups.

Give local residents greater long-term involvement and responsibility for the upkeep of the improved public open spaces. It will be difficult to prevent them becoming degraded once more if the people responsible for preventing that, for example the Council, are not present, as they are not all the time.

Police and community

The ongoing fostering of strong links between police and local residents is critical, not only in matters of day to day crime prevention, but in big operations to amass evidence and catch criminals, and so to remove them from the streets where they can plague local residents. A multi-agency forum like the Colville Area Council is highly beneficial.

Social housing allocations

A fair and equitable mechanism needs to be found by the local authority for continuing to meet need in social housing allocations, as well as to give priority to existing local residents. Many suggestions have been made in numerous reports. What all the suggestions have in common is the need to allocate social housing at the most local level possible, far more local than the entirety of a London borough.

Community regeneration

No regeneration effort can thrive on money alone. Nor can it be sustained solely by self-help and mutual aid, however much they are encouraged through the community activities that are always necessary in regeneration efforts. Altruism, as well as government support, locally and nationally, always has a part to play. Don't set arbitrary time limits for regeneration projects. There may be no exit strategy.

Black and minority ethnic people

It may be necessary to have separate structures as a way of involving black and other minority ethnic people with mainstream decision making. Those structures need to be inclusive and social, as well as formal and business-like. Black people come together not simply to influence or work with mainstream agencies. It is also an important source of mutual aid, social contact for newcomers and mentoring through generations and social classes.

Established support is required from white people in mainstream organisations to establish and sustain black community groups. Staff with confidence and exceptional inter-personal skills are needed to work with black community groups who can bring people together, from all parts of society, without fear or favour and build a relationship of trust. These gifts are more critical than the more prosaic qualities required for mainstream housing management, though they would not go amiss there either.

Local businesses and local people

A new partnership is needed between local residents and local businesses, which are often outposts of much bigger businesses, in the service and retailing sector, to offer well-paid training and employment opportunities for local people in successful global businesses. Community development agencies could facilitate these ties between incoming business and local people. They could also act as key agents of building capacity and enhancing employability. It would retain money earned in the neighbourhood by people living in the neighbourhood. It would also embed the licence to operate of new local businesses. Without that licence to operate they may not survive, as Kassoulet, so stoutly opposed by local people and organisations, found out.

Sustainability

A Mutual Aid Compact should be established to strengthen and sustain the bonds and ties that have grown in the last five years. Without a new focus to take over from City Challenge, commitment could easily dissipate. Residents, households, local agencies and businesses could all be asked to make a commitment to the neighbourhood.

Holistic government

It would be wrong to see these lessons as random, oxymoronic or disconnected. In truth they contain some of the outlines for a new approach to the entire business of national government, an approach which Perri 6 of Demos has called 'holistic government'. He has argued, and the experience of the Colville Project lends much support to these arguments, that holistic government would mean amongst other things:

- Holistic budgeting - budgets should be organised around outcomes and geographical areas, down to level of postcode districts, not by functions or organisations.

- Organisations defined around outcomes.

- Integrated information systems – one-stop shops should become the principal means by which the public deals with the government. One-stop shops would deliver public services organised by life events of citizens.

- Case workers - front line staff should be empowered to purchase services across health, housing, social services, benefits and job training to bring together person-centred packages.

- Enhancing the status and role of preventive work.

- Early warning systems with safeguards.

- Cross-functional outcome measures.

So within the regeneration of one neighbourhood are the ungerminated possibilities of some much needed transformations of government itself.

Learning organisations

I started the book with a description of how our cities are becoming more global, while at the same time the neighbourhoods within them are becoming more like villages, albeit urban villages. I noted the constant need for cities to change and adapt and their ability to throw a shaft of light across humanity's highest hopes, hopes of heaven itself. Cities are homes for the human spirit as well as a home for human lives. But those same changes have degraded cities and the lives of those that live in them. The challenge for us now is to build a set of approaches in local communities, in business and in government that will allow us to make the best of change and remove the worst of it. Our cities are becoming global, but our responses must continue to be local.

We should not underestimate the difficulty of doing this. Resistance to change is great, especially in the public context. As Schon has observed,

> "Established social systems absorb agents of change and dilute and turn to their own end the energies originally directed towards change...When processes embodying threat cannot be repelled, ignored, contained or transformed, social systems tend to respond to change - but the least change capable of neutralising or meeting the intrusive process."

If regeneration initiatives are to go beyond beautifying homes and neighbourhoods, not unworthwhile activities in themselves, and to tackle the so-called 'wicked' issues of crime, poverty and social exclusion; if more emphasis is to be placed on prevention, as well as cure; if we are looking for a social and moral regeneration in which people re-engage with their neighbours and with their neighbourhood, it will not simply be the structure of the regeneration agency that will be critical. It will not simply be a matter of having lots of 108s and lots of Colville-type staff, though that would be a good start. A more comprehensive renewal of organisational processes is needed, in and out of the regeneration neighbourhood.

All of the key players - in the case of Colville, Notting Hill Housing Trust and Kensington Housing Trust, the Royal Borough of Kensington and Chelsea, the Tenant Management Organisation, the police and so on, all of the groups engaged in the Colville Area Council which we described in Chapter two - will have to think of themselves, and indeed become, *learning organisations*. It simply will not do to say "we can change the environment, local people must change and that is that. We, local public service organisations, need learn nothing about our role in these problems arising. Nor have we anything to learn about how we might adapt the way we work in future, in the light of successful efforts (by others) to rectify these problems".

Heaven knows, the means and methods by which the need for renewal and regeneration arose were complex and unpredictable. It will surely follow from that that the means and methods by which we make the necessary changes, and make the changes stick, and then make more changes in the way we work, will also be complex. It will certainly require a commitment to change on the part of all the stakeholders. Professor Nancy Dixon of George Washington University, Washington DC, has written in her book, *Dialogue at Work*, that the learning organisation makes,

> "...intentional use of learning processes at the individual, groups and system level to continuously transform the organisation in a direction that is increasingly satisfying to stakeholders."

It is not for me to say the extent to which this could be said to be true of the stakeholding organisations in Colville. They must answer for themselves. Of some things, however, I am certain. Public service organisations such as schools, health organisations, local authorities, the police and the other emergency services supply the indispensable basis for a civilised society. Yet the pressure to learn and respond to changing needs, demands and circumstances is even greater than in the private sector. The economy may be growing - we are still 'the affluent society' - but the welfare state is shrinking, and the 'grateful generation' which participated in the inception of that idealistic endeavour, are being replaced by far choosier 'customers'. Because the public services did not change themselves, they have been obliged to change through compulsory tendering, outsourcing, local management of schools and the as yet unproven 'best value'. As long as the atmosphere of reluctance and recalcitrance when faced with change pervades the practice of public service, we can be assured that the pressure will not be diminished. It will become more coercive. To use the hackneyed cliché, public service organisations are drinking in the last chance bar. Nor is this pressure confined to the public sector.

Voluntary organisations and the not for profit sector are facing equally challenging times. Some attempt to shoulder the burden of former public services and then, horror-struck, start to manifest many of the bureaucratic, inflexible, uncreative behaviour of the very organisations they took over from. Isomorphism is the ugly term given to this increasingly evident phenomenon. Others spring up in response to new needs almost daily. Faced with overwhelming demands for their services, competition for funds becomes more intense all the time and fundraising becomes more professional. Funding gets skewed to those with the strongest 'brand', not necessarily to those in the greatest need. Everywhere it is all change and if regeneration might mean anything at all, organisations need to be renewed too, and soon.

Chapter ten
To conclude

To cite just one example from the foregoing pages, Notting Hill was probably the most brazenly crime-infested neighbourhood in Britain in 1992. Apart from high levels of 'ordinary' crime – burglaries, street attacks – drugs were openly traded, passers-by were constantly hassled by dealers and prostitutes. Because cities are full of strangers, unsafe streets are the greatest anxiety. So when the neighbourhood was to be regenerated, should the priority have been encouraging local people to co-operate with the police, given the troubled history of murders and riots, or were an ever greater number of security gadgets needed? Both, of course. Regeneration must improve the social and moral atmosphere as well as the physical fabric. Sounds obvious, but hard to deliver.

The Government's Comprehensive Spending Review is complete. Decisions about where to spend future regeneration money, and how, will be taken. The New Deal for Communities has been launched. But, in truth, most regeneration initiatives have disappointed. Buildings, parks and squares are rehabilitated, sometimes temporarily, but tenacious problems remain - unemployment, crime, poor housing, shaky family structures and the abandonment of some neighbourhoods by the private sector and civil society.

City Challenge, Urban Development Corporations, Inner City Task Forces, Safer Cities, Housing Action Trusts, English Partnerships, the Private Finance Initiative and Urban Greening are some Whitehall-initiated programmes. The Single Regeneration Budget brought together 20 sources of funds not a moment too soon. European Structural Funds, with five objectives, are labyrinthine. The logic of this array is obscure. The same people are supposed to benefit from all of them. Each new scheme will supposedly end confusion, stop contradictory policies and respond to all people's needs, not just a piecemeal selection. Expectations have so far outstripped experience. Regeneration is being re-configured by the Government. The Social Exclusion Unit, Regional Development Agencies, Health Action Zones, Education Action Zones, New Deal and others are a Rubik's cube.

City Challenge projects were different from their predecessors. Three main reasons explain their greater effectiveness - structure, outcomes achieved from the expenditure and the neighbourhood base. Herein may be some guiding principles for the expenditure of new funds.

City Challenge projects had their own staff and were independent, at arms length from local authorities. Managers were not distracted by the day to day exigencies of running poorly funded mainstream services. The greater depredations of local government - incompetence, corruption and maladministration - did not afflict them. Partnership working across agencies and functions was the order of the day. Bureaucrats came out of their silos. Combining independence with partnership was a third way.

Bidders for funds did not have to focus on outputs in the past, just needs. Telling funders how unutterably miserable local people were, without practical alternative suggestions, would suffice. City Challenge funds were allocated competitively. Although it took no account of needs and was irksome to the losers, competition encouraged creativity. Even though funding was limited and only available for five years, agencies co-operated in return for, by Government standards, quite small sums. Indeed the financial and time constraints seem to have made people more dynamic. And the public funding levered in private investment, facilitating the private/public funding that the Government wants to see across a bigger canvas.

Previously, money flowed into, for example, setting up voluntary organisations, which collapsed once the tap was turned off. Sustainability has a better chance if services, products and outcomes are clearly defined.

The third success of City Challenge was the neighbourhood base. A local authority area might not seem very big, but it contains many neighbourhoods, many urban villages. The boundaries are not always those of natural communities. Needs are so many and so different that a 'before and after' picture is hard to paint in simple, memorable terms. The alphabet soup of funding initiatives is placed on top of a glutinous stew of statistical indicators. Whereas in a neighbourhood, around a town centre or a high street, all people's needs can be simultaneously held in view. A range of services can come from one place.

Paradoxically some criticised aspects of City Challenge - the five year timescale, the new structures, competition for funds - were effective in defining and delivering an integrated strategy. But there are other criticisms. Firstly, needs-based allocation of funds was absent. Regional Development Agencies should be able to do this sensitively. Secondly, local people and organisations came together to discuss plans to restore houses or parks. However, once works were complete, newly formed connections between people who have been neighbours but strangers for many years, simply fell away. So social regeneration remains elusive; ironic, since the primary motive for spending on regeneration is social - in a prosperous society neighbourhoods should not be so deprived that the conditions of life there are markedly inferior to elsewhere. That is the justification for the Government's welcome focus on social exclusion.

To go back to the example in the neighbourhood with which we are here concerned, improving relations between the police and the community matters far more than spy holes and burglar alarms. Even more important than improving co-operation between local people and agencies is strengthening bonds between residents themselves, building capacity and expanding the full shared innovatory potential of local people. Anything less is a counsel of despair hidden behind newly scrubbed facades.

Funds need to be allocated according to need, but spending decisions need to be taken in neighbourhoods by creative, dedicated staff working across disciplines with many agencies, but at arms length from them all. A clear, published work programme of outputs and deadlines must be followed. There is a challenge for public policy. Transparency and accountability is required when spending public money. Local authorities and NHS trusts are accountable, but too big and distant. Housing associations are too one-dimensional. We need publicly accountable, neighbourhood social regeneration agencies and the Colville Project has taught us a little of how they might work.

Appendix A
Key achievements of the Colville Project

The Colville Urban Regeneration Project was funded by the Department of the Environment City Challenge. The London Borough of Kensington and Chelsea was recognised as the consultative forum for all initiatives in the area and over-saw City Challenge expenditure.

- The Colville Area Council was established to put partnership into action and to give Colville people a voice. Local residents now hold the majority of votes with representation from officers of Notting Hill and Kensington Housing Trusts, Royal Borough of Kensington and Chelsea Tenant Management Organisation, community organisations and the police.

- The Colville Area Residents' Federation successfully campaigned for a local shop to make the Colville Project a focus for residents' activities and aspirations. The Residents' Information Centre (known locally as 108) has since played a central role at the heart of the Colville community.

- The Colville Project undertook major reimprovement works to 127 of Notting Hill Housing Trust's properties – repairs to the external fabric, improved internal layouts, new kitchen and bathroom improvements, noise reduction, central heating and better heat insulation. The Joint Improvement Group was established comprising of Notting Hill staff and tenants to oversee the reimprovement programme, a Tenant Liaison Officer was appointed and tenant information packs were produced in consultation with local residents.

- Energy improvement works were undertaken on 196 Notting Hill Housing Trust homes which included upgrading windows, dry lining, installation and upgrading of heating systems and low energy lighting. The Colville Energy Campaign was developed to help local people to reduce their energy consumption and to heat their homes more affordably.

- Major environmental improvements were made to the area following extensive public consultation. A quiet garden and under-five's play area was created for local use in Colville Square. Improvements to the landscaping and youth facilities were made in Powis Square. In response to a local petition from residents, works were carried out in the Canyon to address a number of long term problems in relation to rubbish storage, traffic management, security and street bleakness.

- Security works were carried out on an additional 254 properties including securing 192 main street front doors resulting in 37 per cent fewer burglaries in the Colville area in 1997 compared with 1992. Steps have also been taken in public spaces to 'design out' crime and anti-social behaviour, such as prostitution, drug dealing and vagrancy.

- An informal approach to tackling local economic problems was adopted using local labour and providing advice and support for businesses and individuals. The Colville Project has helped to set up five local businesses and supported existing community businesses, assisted several residents into jobs and training and helped local residents to win a say in local planning issues.

Bibliography

Abercrombie P and Forshaw J H, *The County of London Plan*, Macmillan, 1943.

Abrahams C, *The Cities: A Methodist report*, NCH Action for Children, 1997.

Argyris C, *Empowerment: The Emperor's New Clothes*, Harvard Business Review, May-June 1998.

Brown N J, (Ed) *Ethics and Agenda 21*, United Nations Environmental Programme, 1994.

Commission on Social Justice, *Social Justice: Strategies for national renewal*, Vintage, 1994.

Dixon N M, *Dialogue at Work: Making talk developmental for people and organizations*, Lemos&Crane, 1998.

Fryer P, *Staying Power: The history of black people in Britain*, Pluto Press, 1984.

Galbraith J K, *The Affluent Society*, Penguin, 1987.

Gilroy P, *The Black Atlantic: Modernity and double consciousness*, Verso, 1993.

Greenhalgh L and Worpole K, *Park Life: Urban parks and social renewal*, Comedia/Demos, 1995.

Hall S, *What is the 'black' in black popular culture?*, Routledge, 1996.

Hobsbawm E, *The Age of Extremes: The short twentieth century 1914 – 1991*, Michael Joseph, 1994.

Landry C and Bianchini F, *The Creative City*, Demos, 1995

Morris J, *Among the Cities*, Penguin, 1985.

Moss Kanter R, *World Class: Thriving globally in the global economy*, Simon and Schuster, 1995.

Mulgan G, *Connexity: How to live in a connected world*, Chatto and Windus, 1997.

Naipaul V S, *The Enigma of Arrival*, Penguin, 1987.

O'Malley J, *The Politics of Community*, Spokesman Books, 1977.

Perri 6, *Escaping Poverty: From safety nets to networks of opportunities*, Demos, 1997.

Porter R, *London: A Social History*, Penguin, 1994.

Rogers R, *Cities for a Small Planet*, Faber and Faber, 1997

Timmins N, *The Five Giants: the history of the Welfare State*, Harper Collins, 1995.

Tomorrow's Company: The role of business in a changing world, RSA Inquiry, 1995.

Townsend P, *A Poor Future*, Lemos&Crane, 1996.

White J and Young M, *Governing London*, Institute of Community Studies, 1996.

Worpole K and Greenhalgh L, *The Freedom of the City*, Demos, 1996.

Young M and Lemos G, *The Communities We Have Lost and Can Regain*, Lemos&Crane, 1997.

Index

108 Bulletin, 23-24

108 Talbot Road. *See* Residents' Information Centre (108 Talbot Road)

Adopt a Tree, 60-61

All Saints Piazza, 59-60

Allocation of social housing, 69-71, 108

Argyris, Chris, 99

Augustine, St, 2

Backdrop of social change, 8

Birth
contact networks through lifecycle, 18

Black and Minority Ethnic Residents Group (BMER), 24, 85-87, 103

Blooming Balconies, 62-63

British Crime Survey, 41-42

Business
local, 94-95, 109-110

Canyon, The, 58-59

Carnival, 83, 87-88

Castells, Manuel, 4-5, 10

Chadwick, Edwin, 8

Cities
making of, 2-3
new role for, 2
political, economic and social shifts, effect of, 2

City Challenge
funding, 13
low-cost security measures, 42
North Kensington, 13-14
paying for 108, 20
programme, 12-13
regeneration initiatives, 45

Cochrane, Kelso, 82, 85, 89

Coins Coffee Shop, 95

Colville Alley, 55

Colville Area Council
AGM at Colville Primary School, 26
formation, 20
membership, 24-26

Colville Area Residents' Forum, 25

Colville estate
1992, in, 11-12
history, 8-9
map, ix
population of ward, 11
walk around, 9-11

Colville Nursery Centre
membership of Colville Area Council, 25-26

Colville Nursery and Primary School, 26, 68

Colville Project
108 as village shop, 17-27
108 integral to success of, 26
home security, 42
impact of, 15-16
key achievements of, 119-120

Colville Square, 54-55

Colville Tavistock Study, 34

Commission on Social Justice, 45

Community involvement
mutual communities. *See* Mutual communities regulation, in, 77-78
structure for, 24, 78-79

Community Land and Workspace Services Ltd (CLAWS), 54

Community Resistance Against Substance Harm (CRASH), 76

Contact networks, 17-18

Crime
  drugs and, 63-66
  home security, 41-43
  joint sting, 66

Death
  contact networks through
  lifecycle, 18

Democratic neighbourhood base,
106-107

Devolution
  government policy, 5

Donnison, David, 13

Drugs
  community action on, 76
  crime, and, 63-66

Earth Summit, Rio de Janeiro, 44

Economy, local. *See* Local economy

Employment
  local labour, 109-110, 94
  training and support of
  residents, 96-97
  See also Local economy

Energy
  efficiency, 43-45
  information, 46-49
  Pinehurst Court, work on, 45-46

Environmental initiatives
  Adopt a Tree, 60-61
  Blooming Balconies, 62-63
  drugs and crime,   63-66
  generally,   60
  joint sting,   66
  Keep Colville Tidy, 62
  learning lessons, 107-108

Ethnicity in Colville, 81

Europe
  antecedents for global cities, 4

Global cities
  development of, 3-5
  meaning, 4

Greenwich
  new village planned for, 7

Heseltine, Michael, MP, 12, 24

History of Colville estate, 8-9

Holistic government, 110-111

Home security, 41-43

Housing
  allocation of social housing,
  69-71, 108
  crisis in 1950s, 32
  improving homes, 107
  Rachmanism, 33
  reimproving homes, 35-37

Housing Action Area
  designation of Colville area as,
  34

Housing Associations as Landlords
Scheme (HALS), 37

Improving homes, 107

Information
  108 Bulletin, 23-24
  energy, on, 46-49

JB's Carwash, 95

Joint Improvement Group
  tenant involvement and, 38-39

Junior League of London, 73-74

Keep Colville Tidy, 62

Kenrick, Revd Bruce, 34

Kensington Housing Trust
  Blooming Balconies
  competition, organisation of,
  62-63
  membership of Colville Area
  Council, 25
  paying for 108, 20

Key achievements of Colville
Project, 119-120

Lawrence, Stephen, 89

Learning organisations, 111-113

Ledbury Road Traffic Campaign,
22, 77, 103

Lee, Laurie, 30

Lifecycle
  contact networks through, 18

Livingstone, Sonia, 29

Local economy
  Coins Coffee Shop, 95
  future, 97-98
  JB's Carwash, 95
  local business, 94-95, 109-110
  local labour, 109-110, 94
  Marios, 95
  regeneration, 109, 115-118
  setting up 108, 96
  swapping power, 96
  training and support of residents, 96-97
  village divided, 91-94

Local involvement. *See* Community involvement

London
  global city, as, 4
  location, 3
  Mayor for, 5
  population, 3
  qualities of, 3

London School of Economics, 29-30

Map of Colville estate, ix

Marios, 95

Metropolitan Police. *See* Notting Hill Police

Millennium Dome, 7

More, Thomas, 1

Morris, Jan, 1

Mulgan, Geoff, 2

Multi-Cultural History Week
  local support for, 20, 87-88

Mutual aid
  Compact, 110, 99-104
  external commitment, 99-100
  internal commitment, 100
  nature of, 71-73

Mutual communities
  allocation of social housing, 69-71
  drugs, community action on, 76
  generally, 67
  Junior League of London, 73-74

Ledbury Road Traffic Campaign, 77
  mutual aid, 71-73
  neighbourhood safety, 74-75
  Pimento, 73
  police and community, 74, 108
  regulation, local involvement in, 77-78
  stability of residence, 67-69
  structure for community involvement, 78-79
  Vicarage site, 75

Neighbourhood
  Adopt a Tree, 60-61
  All Saints Piazza, 59-60
  around, 51-53
  Blooming Balconies, 62-63
  Canyon, 58-59
  Colville, 53-54
  Colville Alley, 55
  Colville Square, 54-55
  democratic neighbourhood base, 106-107
  drugs and crime, 63-66
  environmental initiatives, 60
  joint sting, 66
  Keep Colville Tidy, 62
  open spaces, 51-53
  Powis Square, 56-57
  safety, 74-75

Newsletter
  108 Bulletin, 23-24

North Kensington City Challenge
  launch, 13
  nature of, 13-14
  objectives, 14

Northern Ireland
  devolution, 5

Notting Hill Housing Trust
  energy efficiency, 44-45
  establishment of, 34-35
  membership of Colville Area Council, 25
  paying for 108, 20
  staff of Colville Project based at offices of, 19

Notting Hill Police
  community, police and, 108 74
  crime prevention, 42

drugs and crime, 64-66
  joint sting, 66
  learning lessons, 108
  membership of Colville Area
    Council, 25
  neighbourhood safety, 74-75

O'Malley, Jan, 33

Opening 108, 20-21

Paying for 108, 20

Pimento
  activities of, 73

Pinehurst Court, 45-46

Police. *See* Notting Hill Police

Porter, Roy, 8-9, 11

Poverty and deprivation, 91-92

Powell, Enoch, 32

Powis Square, 56-57

Private space
  changing use of, 29-32

Public space
  changing use of, 29-32

Race
  arrival and losing gift of dreams,
    82
  BMER, 85-87, 24
  black and minority ethnic
    people, 109
  diversity, 83-85
  ethnicity of Colville, 81
  generally, 81
  inclusion, 85
  learning lessons, 109
  Multi-Cultural History Week,
    20, 87-88
racial hatred, continuing
    presence of, 89
  recognising change, 88-89
  scars on soul, 82
  struggle, 83

Rachman, Perec, 33

Re-opening of village shop, 19-20

Regeneration, 109, 115-118

Regulation
  local involvement in, 77-78

Reimproving homes, 35-37

Residence
  stability of, 67-69

Residents' Information Centre
    (108 Talbot Road)
  108 Bulletin, 23-24
  background, 19-20
  opening, 20-21
  paying for, 20
  services from, 21-23
  setting up 108, 96
  structure for community
    involvement, 24
  success of, 26-27

Rogers, Richard, 43

Royal Borough of Kensington and
Chelsea
  home security, joint initiative
    on, 42
  membership of Colville Area
    Council, 25
  paying for 108, 20

Safety
  neighbourhood, 74-75

Schools
  Colville Area Council and,
    26
  nursery, 68-69
  Pimento, 73
  primary, 68-69
  stability of residence and,
    68-69

Scotland
  devolution, 5

Scott, Giles Gilbert, 10

Security
  concerns about, 41-43
  neighbourhood safety, 74-75

Services from 108, 21-23

Setting up 108, 96

Single Regeneration Budget, 24

Social change
  backdrop of, 8

Social Exclusion Unit, 5

Social housing
  allocation of, 69-71 108

St Mary of Angels School, 68

St Stephen's School, 68

Stability of residence, 67-69

Structure for community
  involvement, 24, 78-79

Sustainability, 110

Swapping power, 96

Tenant involvement
  Joint Improvement Group,
  38-39

Tenant liaison officer
  functions of, 40-41

Tenants' management organisation
(TMO)
  membership of Colville Area
  Council, 25

Tickell, Sir Crispin, 7

Training and support of residents,
96-97

Trustafarians
  meaning, 10

Urban villages
  nature of, 5-7

Vicarage site, 75

Vicissitudes of time, 1-2

Village shop
  108 Talbot Road as, 17-27
  contact networks, 17-18
  re-opening of, 19-20

Wales
  devolution, 5

Walk around Colville estate, 9-11

Walsall
  structure for community
  involvement, 24

Women's Education in Building
(WEB)
  refurbishment of 108, 20, 94

Wonder, Stevie, 5